D0992924

First and Second Kings, Maurice and Harold

*The True Story of Eccentric Millionaires
Who Lived Like Paupers*

Selected books by Mary-Jo Burles

Cabin Creek Ranch: 100 Years on the Homestead
Julia's Gift: Her Life, Her Poems
Family Favourites
Be My Guest

For Children

The Christmas Camel
Jean and the Happy Voice
Give a Llama to Your Grandma
Grandfather Clock Takes a Holiday
Elfreda, the Elf, Goes to the North Pole
Daisy, the Duck Who Couldn't Swim
The Squirrel Who Wouldn't Jump
Boo, the Little Blue Ghost
Little Poky's Easter Task
Robbie Robin's Return

With Marjorie Haugen

Cowley: 60 Years a Village, 1906-1966

FIRST AND SECOND KINGS, MAURICE AND HAROLD

*The True Story of Eccentric Millionaires
Who Lived Like Paupers*

by Mary-Jo Burles

HBLS

First edition 2000
Second edition 2002
Third edition 2007
Fourth edition 2008
Second printing 2010

HBLS, 15-47470 Chartwell Drive,
Chilliwack, British Columbia V2P 8A2 Canada
Email: hblsbooks@gmail.com
Website: www.hblsbooks.com

Library and Archives Canada Cataloguing in Publication
Burles, Mary-Jo, 1927–2009
    First and second Kings, Maurice and Harold : the true story of eccentric
        millionaires who lived like paupers / Mary-Jo Burles.—4th ed.

    ISBN 978-0-9783192-2-9

1. King, Maurice, 1897-1996. 2. King, Harold, 1899-1995. 3. Porcupine
Hills (Alta.)—Biography. 4. Pioneers—Alberta—Porcupine Hills—Biography.
5. Millionnaires—Alberta—Biography. 6. Eccentrics and eccentricities—
Alberta—Biography. I. Title.

FC3695.P67Z49 2008   971.23'4020922   C2008-904330-8

Cover photograph by Lowell Aldrich
Author photograph by Lloyd Knight
Design by Momentum Productions • www.momentumproductions.net
Printed and bound in Canada

*To Dr. Clarence Smith
who is responsible for
this book's having
been written.*

*Without frugality none can be rich,
and with it very few would be poor.*
—*Samuel Johnson*

Contents

ACKNOWLEDGMENTS

I must first thank my husband Bob, for all the time he spent cutting paper at the kitchen table, running errands for me and for his patience when my mind was with Maurice and Harold rather than on what I was doing at the moment. It was much appreciated. Thanks also for taking on some of the daily household chores so I would have more time to work.

Thanks also to the many people who contributed their stories to this book, people who knew the King Brothers well and shared their information—Ronald Nelson, Rachel Dwyer, Virginia Delinte, and Willie Thibert and Peter Demosky, Orrin Hart and others. You know who you are.

Special thanks to the late Rosella Thibert and my mother Laurell Sweeney, the two women who made me keep writing every time I wanted to quit.

Thank you also to Lloyd Knight of Lethbridge who granted me permission to use the wonderful picture of Maurice, Harold, and Bill Lagarde.

Thanks also to the family of the late Gray Campbell who had the picture in their possession and who sent it to me after Gray died.

My thanks also to Diane Aldrich for permission to use that

wonderful picture of Maurice and Harold taken by her husband Lowell Aldrich, the picture that placed in the top ten of the Smithsonian competition in the people's category.

A big thank you to Dr. Clarence Smith, our former veterinarian and friend who prodded me into starting this book.

Special thanks to my daughter Heather for her encouragement and to my other daughter Jacquelyn who acted as my long distance computer consultant and kept my printer printing when its icon disappeared from the screen or behaved oddly.

Without you all, I could not have done it. Thank you!

FIRST AND SECOND KINGS, MAURICE AND HAROLD

The True Story of Eccentric Millionaires
Who Lived Like Paupers

INTRODUCTION

A funny thing happened on the way to Jerusalem this September of the year 2000. I had almost finished a rough draft of this book about the two King Brothers, Maurice and Harold, but I could not settle on a title for it. At least ten had run through my mind and I rejected them all as not quite right.

Then, some place between Nazareth and Jerusalem, I was telling Ruth Mack, the wife of the Anglican minister who was our tour conductor, a true story about the time I read First Corinthians 13, the Hymn of Love from the New Testament of the Bible, at my youngest daughter's wedding. After the ceremony, my sister-in-law came up to me and said, "Mary-Jo, that was just beautiful. Did you write it yourself?" As I started to answer, my cousin, a Queen's Court lawyer who was standing close by, said, "No, she didn't write it. Our grandfather did." I guess it must have sounded familiar to him and as my grandfather wrote poetry, he assumed I had borrowed it.

Ruth is a minister's wife so I knew she had more than a nodding acquaintance with the Bible and would understand the story. We had a good laugh over it and later she came up to me and said, "What about the Psalms? Did you write them?" I disclaimed any credit for the Psalms as well as for First Corinthians 13, and then added lightly, "But I did write First and Second Kings."

We both laughed and I added, "But the first and second Kings I wrote about were Maurice and Harold King who lived in abject poverty all their lives while accumulating a fortune in land."

That night when I went to bed I thought that *First and Second Kings, Maurice and Harold* might be a good title for this book. And that is how it came to be.

Chapter 1

GETTING STARTED

They were not much more than boys when they left home for good, only to return for occasional visits to their mother on the east side of the ridge. "The ridge" is the line of hills which divide the Porcupines, the foothills just east of the Livingstone Range of the Rocky Mountains, into east and west. On the east side of the ridge is the town of Claresholm, the business centre, and on the west side it is a long 35 to 40 mile trip south to Pincher Creek. The Porcupine Hills, or the "Porkies" as they are widely known, have some of the best grazing land for cattle in all of Canada and it was here that Maurice and Harold, the King Brothers, finally settled.

"I think they were about 19 and 20 when they came to this side to work," recalled Bill Lagarde who hunted with them and was one of their best friends. "They had five dollars between them and a few dollars worth of grub and that was how they got their start. They was tough and they made it. They walked all the way and they had water for lunch."

They lived under canvas at first—not a real tent but a tarpaulin rigged up as a shelter—or they stayed in a vacant shack. Either way, the temperature was as cold inside as it was out.

They did not have down-filled sleeping bags, but they

survived. Occasionally they sheltered in someone's barn, perhaps on a rare occasion in someone's home but it would have been rarely, because most houses were small, and families were large, and there were the two of them, which meant they would need a bed to themselves. As their friend Bill said, "They were tough."

They were proud and would not impose. Not being beholden was their credo in life. They had accepted charity often and it may have been a bitter pill at times. "It's better to give than to receive," Maurice was fond of saying, and then would add, "and it's even better to have something to give than to have to be on the receiving end."

Later in life they remembered what it was to have been dirt poor and offered kindness when they could. In some respects it made them hard, but they never forgot the people they owed. They had learned early in life that they could not depend on their parents or many others and that they had only each other. In their home, later in life, no one was ever turned away from shelter and food. They took in all kinds of strays and often paid them wages to boot. They would have found a corner and a blanket of some sort for any stranger at the door. They willingly shared what they had in their home but sometimes it wasn't much.

When they came over the ridge from Claresholm they also had an old rifle and some old traps. "I think somebody gave them to them. And it weren't the last time they had water for lunch, by a long shot," added Bill who knew the brothers better than most.

Chapter 2

WHAT WERE THEY WORTH?

Maurice and Harold King, eccentric bachelor millionaire brothers, as the newspaper reporters called them after they had both died, were a legend in their lifetimes, known far and wide for their Spartan lifestyle and the amount of land they owned. People liked to guess as to what the brothers were worth and what they owned. Often the brothers weren't quite sure themselves how much they had at any given moment because Maurice was always buying, selling or trading. Also, Maurice was always cagey at letting anybody know exactly what they did have. "Well, I think it's quite a bit" was a common answer when someone tried to quiz him about his holdings after he was known to be rich.

"But I couldn't exactly tell you 'cause I don't reckon I know exactly myself." Maybe he didn't, but their estate sold for more than six million dollars after he died, and made headlines in the eastern papers as well as those in the West. It was said to be the biggest land sale in Canadian ranching history.

Stories from early neighbours said that when they did make a little money as boys, their father took it for drink, so Maurice learned early in life to keep his own counsel. "If they don't know you have it," he said to me once, "then they can't take it away from you."

Chapter 3

THE REASONS BEHIND THIS BOOK

*T*hey may have been cash poor and land rich while they lived but they were worth a lot in later years. A number of articles had been published about them in numerous western papers and magazines while they lived. Some were closer to the truth than others. Some just capitalized on their eccentricities.

"They knew some of the stories that were told about them," said Eve, their foreman's wife, "and they even contributed to them. They never had a pair of dogs but one story going the rounds was that they never washed dishes but had two dogs who licked the plates clean." Another popular story had Maurice buttering a slice of bread in front of company and then turning to his brother to say, "See if there's a mouse in one of those traps, will you? I could slice it on for sandwich meat." It was not a true story, in that Maurice never ate a mouse sandwich, but after seeing how they lived, I'm sure many people believed it to be true. The bear stories were true.

I had never considered writing about Kings while they were alive. I never seriously thought about writing about them after they were dead, either, not even after several people suggested it or asked me if I were. I never thought of them as odd. I thought of them as friends, two of the first friends I had in Alberta and two of the best.

But one night over coffee after a Museum meeting in Pincher Creek, our former vet, Dr. Clarence Smith, who had visited Maurice and Harold as often as he had us, looked at the picture of the two old-timers hanging on the wall of the Waldron house living room where we were holding our meeting.

There they were, grizzled heads and flannel shirts, staring out from Lowell Aldrich's photograph of them in their last years, as big as life. "Have you started a book about them yet?" Clarence asked me. I shook my head and he said, "Somebody should and you're the one to do it. You knew them better than most people."

I hesitated for a few seconds as I thought about what he had said and then agreed. "You're right," I said, "I did know them better than most and maybe I am the one to do it."

"I know you are," said Clarence and before I left that night I had verbally committed myself to writing this book, a biographical sketch of two men who had lived their lives as best they could, going by the teachings of the Bible and clinging to old-fashioned virtues like honesty, thrift and their personal integrity in an ever changing world. To Maurice, a handshake to seal a deal was as good as a legal, witnessed document drawn up by a team of lawyers.

Much has been omitted from this story—things about which I was doubtful and things I did not see fit to include.

Chapter 4

THE PERSONAL SIDE

*O*nce a reporter who was doing a feature story on the brothers while they were alive said, "You must pretty well agree on most things to be able to live together as long as you have." Maurice thought about that one a minute and then said, "Nope! Can't rightly say we do. Don't reckon I can think of a time when we agreed on anything." It was true. Whether they ever had a verbal agreement to disagree or not, they must have agreed to disagree at one time and having that out of the way, they just lived and let live. They had silently mastered the art of compromise.

So this is a personal account of two men I liked and their influence on the people around them and my family's relationship with them over the years. Harold enjoyed making puns on their name. He would often shove his chair back from the table after a good meal and say, "Now that was a meal fit for a king." And now I add one to his collection—we would not have many bankruptcies or farm foreclosures if we all lived like Kings.

Other people have contributed stories and memoirs of their dealings with the King Brothers, too. Often we shared a good laugh as we swapped stories about them, but always there was

Glenbow Archives, NA-2864-24350-17

Maurice King said he couldn't think of a time when he and his brother Harold agreed on anything.

a grudging respect for the two old men who had marched to the beat of a different drum.

I miss them still—the genuine welcome they always had for us, and their way of looking at life, politics and religion. I often thought their attitudes a bit naive but always genuine—they had no guile. They were good and I thought they often brought out the good in others, even if it came out reluctantly. True goodness is in itself unusual. I knew they weren't perfect and so did they, and we accepted each other as such.

Chapter 5

MY FIRST MEETING WITH KINGS

*M*aurice and Harold King were two of the first people I met when I came to the Porcupine Hills of southern Alberta to teach school in the fall of 1949. Marcel Dejax, the school trustee for Olin Creek, the small rural school I had accepted while on a summer vacation in Alberta, was a good friend of the King boys. Marcel hid his amusement at my appearance (I was dressed in the latest fashion for Winnipeg but not for rural Alberta) as he helped me into a truck that had seen better days and I hid my sheer terror at the perilous hills and coulees as we rattled our way to his home where I was to board. Back home these hills we were driving through would have been called mountains.

Annie, Marcel's wife, who became a good friend, greeted me warmly and was interested in my garb, demanding to know as she showed me to my room if long ankle length flared skirts and lace trimmed blouses were the style "back east". I assured her that they were, even as I realized they were slightly out of place here. I also realized that while we in Manitoba had always thought of ourselves as part of Western Canada, these people looked on us as part of the East.

This was the first log house I had ever seen. The interior was finished with wall board and it was a comfortable, scrupulously clean home. I learned in due time that there were many log houses and barns and other buildings in this part of the country. Logs were not only handy but they were cheap.

If I had not been boarding with Marcel and Annie Dejax I might not have met the King Brothers that first fall. But scarcely two weeks of that first school month had gone by when Marcel announced that he and his son, ten-year-old Jimmie, one of my students, were going to visit their friends, the Kings, and would I like to come. I wasn't sure whether I wanted to meet them or not, but Annie got into the act and insisted that I go to see what she called "two of the most eligible bachelors in the country." I knew by the way she laughed as she said it that there was more to it than met the eye.

"You must meet them," she insisted. I had exchanged my long skirt and frilly blouse for grey wool slacks and a matching sweater over a cotton blouse, and more sensible shoes, before I got in the truck this time. I did not know it yet, but the passenger gets to open gates, wire gates, and Jimmie was comfortably wedged in the middle so the job fell to me. I had never opened a wire gate before and there were several wire gates (it seemed like at least a hundred) as well as a big wooden one before we got to the King house. Opening the wire gates had been difficult but I had managed, although the barbs in one had torn my expensive slacks. Many Westerners took real pride in making a wire gate so tight a strong man could barely undo it.

The last gate, a large wooden one almost at the King house, was beyond me. The ground was spongy and I hopped from one foot to the other to save my good shoes and finally Marcel got out of the truck to come to my help. We had bounced over a good ten or twelve miles of dirt roads with rocks poking through every

The King Ranch house near Sharples Creek in the Porcupine Hills.

foot of the way to get to Sharples Creek where we had wound down a long, steep curving hill to get to the wooden gate. So I arrived at Kings frustrated at my own incompetence and annoyed over the rip in my pants.

I could not hide it and Maurice was openly amused when he heard how I had wrecked my good clothing. I'm sure he thought it served me right for not wearing the tough blue jeans which were almost a uniform for both sexes in southern Alberta. The King Brothers both wore blue jeans for every day and for dress all the days of their lives.

Chapter 6

A BACHELOR ESTABLISHMENT

*B*ack home I had visited bachelor establishments when I travelled the countryside with my grandfather who had sold them their land in Manitoba. I had seen rural poverty but I had never seen anything like this.

It must have been a better than average home at one time, a two-storey log house. We entered directly into the kitchen and we stayed there. In many country homes the kitchen was the most used room, or almost the only one, of the house and it was true here. In all the times I visited them, we never once sat in the living room, but always around the kitchen table.

There was a living room off to the right and much later, once when Maurice asked me to get something from there, I saw that a staircase against one wall led to the second floor and their sleeping quarters. Virginia creeper vines had crept through the holes and cracks where the chinking had fallen out of the log walls. The vines almost covered the one small, dirty window. I think it was a standard size window but it had so many things piled in front of it only the top pane could be seen.

The kitchen, with its rough board floor and utensils and pans hanging from nails on the walls, was simple. A crude washstand stood against an outside wall and a tin basin with a dirty pool of

31

water in its bottom sat on the washstand. This was customary in many farm homes where every ounce of water had to be carried or "packed" as they said. You didn't throw it out until it was close to mud. A small piece of soap sat by the basin and an old hand towel, as dirty as the water in the basin, hung from a corner of the washstand. When I washed my hands there before starting to cook an hour or so later, I merely dipped my fingertips into the water and even more gingerly dried them on the rag. Maurice remembered and many years later smiled as he said, "Once we had a lady visitor who thought the towel was too dirty to use." I merely smiled. I doubt that I was the only one who felt mild revulsion at the thought of drying my hands on that dirty rag of a towel.

The rough wooden table was littered with leftover scraps of food and dirty plates and over it all swarmed the flies, hundreds of hungry houseflies. Other people have made the remark that they never once saw the table cleared—that it was always littered with the remains of the last meal. And so it was, almost always, but at least once it was cleared and set with a white cloth. That story comes later.

The huge cook stove, a wood and coal burning range, sat in one corner of the room opposite the door. A few rough shelves held water pails and other items. The inevitable slop pail for waste water was on the floor somewhere between the washstand and the stove. The rest of the furniture consisted of rough wooden crates and boxes which had once held apples or oranges before being put to use as storage units. The brothers had all the necessities and they were duplicated in many other country homes. They were crude, they were cheap, and they served the purpose.

The two men stood up as we entered the room and shook hands with me as Marcel introduced me. Maurice's handshake was firm but normal, but Harold took my hand in his and pumped my arm as he squeezed my hand until I thought the bones would break. This was a typical handshake for Harold. Even in old age he had a stronger grip than most men ever had. Shaking hands with Harold King was a challenge.

We sat around the table on wooden chairs, some minus their backs. Marcel and "the boys", Maurice and Harold, who were close to an age, chatted about cattle and crops, fishing and weather, and there was an occasional glance in my direction but I was not included in the conversation. This, I learned later, was typical. Women were to be seen but not heard and segregation of the sexes at parties and gatherings was traditional. However, my first impression of Maurice and Harold King, and it was a lasting one, was their deferential courtesy. It was their attitude towards most women.

I think Maurice would have paid respect to the lowest prostitute as I often heard him say that the man who employed her for sexual use was far worse than she was. I'm sure he believed what he said, that they should put the men in jail rather than the women. It was an unusual view for a man to hold and I often thought he was far ahead of his time.

I would like to have browsed through the huge pile of *The Saturday Evening Post* and *Country Gentleman* (two of the best known magazines of the day) that were heaped up on a cupboard at one side of the room but I was too shy to ask. Maurice and Harold were both well read and kept up on current events through magazines like this and with the radio. They never had television until their last few years when they lived with their foreman and his wife.

So while they talked, I amused myself by looking at the ancient calendars on the walls. It seemed that they never took one down—they just hung a new one on top of the old ones. Some of them dated back to the pin-up pictures of the thirties or earlier.

After talking about fishing, crops, hunting and cattle for an hour or two, Maurice announced that we would stay for supper. He didn't invite us, he told us. Marcel agreed, and then I discovered another western custom. Since I was the only woman present, I would do the cooking. It was just taken for granted. I had been cooking for years but not under conditions like these.

They put another stick or two of wood in the cook stove and stirred it up to a blaze. Maurice brought out the biggest, thickest beef steak I had ever set eyes on. It must have been close to an inch thick. Maurice took the front lid off the stove and pointed to the huge cast-iron frying pan which was heating up on the stove. The frying pan went into the hole left when the front lid had been removed and temporarily set aside on top of the back of the stove.

Beef steak was a luxury to town people like me and when we did buy steaks they were smaller and thinner than this one. Steak was expensive and in my home my mother would never trust anyone else to cook it. I had watched her and listened to her long enough to pick up the basics but I was terrified that I would make a mess of it. One of the cardinal sins was not cooking the steak right—it had to be seared on the outside and rare in the inside. This one turned out to be rare, all right, the rarest I have ever seen.

When the grease in the crusted old frying pan was sizzling, I threw in the whole steak. Grease splattered all over the place and I waited for the better part of two minutes, stuck a fork in the meat—tongs were unheard of—turned it over and let it sizzle for another two minutes. Then I put it on a heavy platter Maurice had set out. I think we had boiled potatoes along with the steak

Maurice and Harold finishing dinner at the King Ranch in 1973.

but I don't think I ate any. We just shoved the dirty dishes from the previous meal to one end of the table and fell to it. The steak was blood red in the middle but well seared on the outsides.

Marcel told me later that Maurice liked his steak cooked that way, but the sight of all that blood almost made Jimmie sick at his stomach. Annie told me later that I had endeared myself to Maurice for life. Never much of a meat eater, I nibbled away at a small corner of my share and brushed the flies back. After the meal we heated clean water in the dishpan and I washed dishes. Harold dried the dishes for me but it would have been more sanitary to let them drip dry. The tea towel was not the cleanest I had ever seen. It and the hand towel appeared to have been washed about the same time.

Chapter 7

TO SMOKE OR NOT TO SMOKE

After that first dinner, Harold tried to teach me how to roll a cigarette with Bull Durham tobacco. Bull Durham is very fine tobacco and difficult to roll. The result is often a little twisted cigarette paper with a wee bit of tobacco held in the middle by the twists. After having a good laugh at my efforts, he rolled one for me and then tried to teach me again. I never did get very good at it, at least not with Bull Durham which Harold always used. He was a heavy smoker and a lifelong smoker although Maurice tried to get him to quit.

Since Harold could climb the steepest hills at a gallop and without stopping to draw a breath, he didn't pay much attention to his brother. Maurice worried about his brother's bad habit and said to me once or twice, "I tried to get 'The Boss' to quit smoking but he don't listen." I don't believe that Harold smoked tailor-made cigarettes often—they would have cost too much and it would have been too easy to run out of them when they were that far from town. There was so little tobacco in his Bull Durham cigarettes that I don't think they did him any harm.

They called each other "The Boss" and I expect they both took turns at it, so the name fit them both.

That was my introduction to the two brothers, Maurice and Harold King, who lived most of their long lives north of Cowley in the Porcupine Hills of Southern Alberta and died there, too, at close to one hundred. They must have been sneaking up on fifty then, and to a twenty year old they were ancient. After they had both died, Eve Hoffman, their foreman's wife, showed me snapshots of them at the age they must have been when I first met them. They were nice-looking men and didn't look at all old, but I never ever thought of them as eligible bachelors.

But then again, I never thought of them as that eccentric, either.

Chapter 8

MAURICE, HAROLD, AND JESUS

Mostly this story is about Maurice, although the two of them, he and his brother, were inseparable in most people's minds. My husband and I saw Maurice more often than we did his quieter, shier brother and he was easier to talk to than Harold, or Rold, or Raoul, as they called him. At least I found him so.

Maurice handled the business dealings and banking so he got out more while Harold stayed home and tended the garden or went hunting or fishing. I liked them both and admired them, but it was mostly Maurice with whom I had long conversations about politics, economics, religion and even sex, although I thought Harold was more deeply and quietly religious than his older brother.

"You can't tell me Jesus died for my sins," Harold would argue. "I'm responsible for my own and he died long before I was born, so how can he even know what I did and how can he be responsible for mine?" Maurice disagreed, having, as the popular saying goes, accepted Jesus Christ as the mediator. I tried to stay out of their ongoing argument. I thought they had both made their points—that one is responsible for one's own actions, as Harold said, but after recognizing Jesus as the

Saviour, as Maurice pointed out, one could cast one's burdens on him, because he had accepted the scapegoat role willingly.

Chapter 9

ECONOMY

Maurice was a shrewd man. Both men were philosophers who knew and understood the teachings of the Bible and also the way governments work. "Once you understand human nature," Maurice was fond of saying, "then you know that there is no hope for the world unless man changes himself. He can't improve the world until he does that. And in my opinion, he ain't likely to do that." Maurice was fond of prefacing or finishing his remarks by saying, "And in my opinion." One could disagree with his opinion but one had to admit his right to have it. The Jehovah Witnesses used to visit him and he quite enjoyed their visits and the discussions they had.

Over the years I learned a lot from both men. Often when faced with a dilemma, I would ask myself, "What would Maurice say?" Most of the time the answer was that he would probably say, "Well, if you can afford it, all right, but if you can't, then maybe you could do without." His opinion was important to me although, having children to consider, I wanted a better standard of living than they had. They both practised and preached economy, not to go into debt for things we could do without, how to "make do" with what we had and how to decide what was important and what wasn't.

In Spartan living they were not alone. The countryside was full of abandoned houses and stories of people who had come and gone. They were the ones who had not practised thrift and economies, or who were not willing to live dirt cheap. Most of the ones who were still here or who were passing their places on to the next generation had never lived very "high on the hog".

Neither Maurice nor Harold judged people by how well dressed they were or how new their cars, although Maurice once said to me it was a treat to see a well turned out woman—one who dressed nicely. But I'm sure he didn't mean expensively. I don't think they often judged people harshly—they just accepted them. Neither did they expect to be judged by other people's standards. Maurice in particular mistrusted people who put on a good front when he suspected that a front was all it was.

One of his favourite sayings, and he had many, was "Show me a man with two suits and I'll show you a man who has no money of his own in the pockets." Or, "Show me a man driving a new car and I'll show you a man with no money in the bank and a car not paid for."

I don't believe they ever owned a car but they did abandon the horse and buggy era and buy a truck. A car, used over the rough roads they had, would not have lasted long and it was not a necessity. A truck was, but Maurice kept track of every penny spent to run it. Their truck was usually in fair condition as Maurice considered it good economy to have a vehicle that wasn't always broken down, but they still used the saddle horse for many local trips.

As far as farm machinery was concerned, it was mostly old, acquired second-hand and repaired until it was no longer possible to do so. Ray Scotton remembers going up to try to fix an old John Deere tractor that had seen better days. "He'd had it all to pieces," said Ray. "We worked on it a long time and talked while we worked, and it came out that just about everybody in the country had worked on that old tractor and couldn't get it going. I wondered if maybe he'd dropped a piece or two in the grass but he swore it was all there."

More than once we had Russell or another of Maurice's men come to our place to phone to tell him that the haying equipment had broken down again.

Chapter 10

IN SICKNESS AND HEALTH

*T*heir lifestyle certainly seems to have been a healthy one for them. Both men lived to be almost a hundred. In later years they were once hospitalized for pneumonia and when I went to see them as they lay in Pincher Creek Hospital wearing white hospital gowns and all shaved and cleaned, I thought they would probably never go home again. Harold joked about having been scrubbed within an inch of his life. "By golly," he said, "I'm squeaky clean." This amused my husband and I heard him repeat it over and over, "I'm squeaky clean." It is an old saying and an accurate description stemming from having your head washed until the hair was so soap free and clean that it would literally squeak.

But they did recover and go home and lived for several years after that. They were tough old birds. They did have prostrate problems, too, but got over them and were rarely ill, enjoying relatively good health, considering their ages. Towards the last Harold was ready to die and wanted to die. Often he would say, "I don't know why I'm still alive," and we knew he wished he weren't. He had never cared much about accumulating the land that Maurice wanted so badly. Often he would say, "Why bother?" Now they had no use for the money they were worth and Harold took little pleasure or satisfaction in it.

Another time when I visited them in hospital in Pincher Creek, they lay so quietly in side-by-side beds in the same room and were so subdued I didn't think either one of them would live. Both of them made it that time, too. As their friend Bill had said, "They were tough." One of the nurses told me that every night Maurice was in the hospital, he got down on his knees to say his prayers.

Once when I visited them in Claresholm Hospital I was embarrassed. It was a quiet Sunday afternoon and by this time Maurice was deafer than ever so that our conversation was carried on at a shout. He insisted on talking about his favourite topics—politics, religion, and sex from a Scriptural angle. Somewhere in our discourse, Harold got out of bed, pulled on a hospital robe, shoved his feet into carpet slippers and shuffled away and left us to it. I was hoarse from yelling at Maurice by the time we left and as we walked down the long corridor to the exit, I wondered why a nurse hadn't come in to tell us to be a little quieter. I was quite sure that everybody in the hospital—patients, staff and visitors—knew my views on politics, religion and sex.

Maurice was determined to outlive his brother. He was afraid Harold might give everything away. Harold, in Maurice's opinion, was much too soft with people. This is ironic, because the lengthy lawsuit over their home quarter on Sharples Creek arose because of a verbal statement Maurice allegedly made to a woman they had allowed to live in a shack on their property. She claimed after his death that Maurice had told her she could live there always and filed a claim for ownership. A lawyer phoned me one day to see if I could shed any light on the matter but all I could say was that it didn't sound like Maurice to promise anybody anything. I thought he might have told her that she could live there as long as he was alive, but it seemed strange to me that she was the only one who ever heard him say anything about the length of her tenancy at all.

Nobody else had heard him promise her anything, although it was apparently true that he spent many afternoons visiting with the woman who lived in their shack.

How did she get there? One of the neighbours ran into her when she was lost and looking for someone who might pasture her horses for her. He sent her to Maurice and we are eternally grateful that he didn't send her to us. Since the woman claimed the horses were worth more than one hundred thousand dollars, one wonders why she didn't sell a horse or two and move to a more comfortable home. The shack which Maurice let her use was not deluxe accommodation. With no electricity, no heat, and no plumbing it would have been more suitable for a summer cottage. Indeed, someone told me that she often went either to B.C. or to California for the winters. One can only assume she was living on there in hopes and expectations.

She claimed also that they spent their afternoons together reading the Bible and that Maurice taught her how to read and interpret it. I have no doubt that they spent hours on his favourite book, but since Maurice was close to blind, he couldn't have done much of the reading.

After a court case he had lost, a few years earlier, because it was a verbal agreement, he was even cagier than he had been in earlier years. There wasn't a word about the woman in any of his wills and by this time he was putting things in writing. He had begun to realize that not every man's word is his bond.

When Maurice died in 1996, Harold having preceded him in 1995, they made headlines in newspapers all over the country and were labelled "Eccentric Millionaire Bachelor Brothers". The headlines were not accurate as their executor pointed out. They were not millionaires while they were alive. They may have been worth millions but they did not *have* millions. As the old saying says, they were "land rich and cash poor".

During their lifetimes they had accumulated prime ranch land which sold at auction for several million dollars although for most of their lives they had lived in what can only be described as abject poverty. For many years it was from necessity and after that probably from force of habit until failing health in their last years forced them to move in with their foreman and his wife, Russell and Eve Hoffman. Maurice, who made most of the financial decisions, had taken a long time and only reluctantly provided decent housing for his foreman and family, but now he was reaping the benefits of it himself.

Eve Hoffman made a good home for them and looked after them well. Eve preferred country life to living in town and never minded the isolation. She was a quiet person and an excellent cook as well as a superb, though unlicensed nurse. She just seemed to be naturally good at whatever she did and was happy with her garden and her poultry and her family.

Sometimes, when I saw how comfortable Maurice and Harold were at Hoffman's they reminded me of two old alley cats who had come in out of the cold and couldn't quite believe their luck. Prior to their moving in with their foreman, Eve had made two trips a day to the old house on Sharples Creek to put drops in Harold's eyes. She was a good nurse.

Maurice had kept them on after Russell was unable to work. Russell had an allergy so that he could not handle hay or even work around it. It affected his lungs and breathing badly.

I think the brothers didn't want to lose Eve.

Chapter 11

THOUGHTS ON HIRED HELP

O ver the years they had seen a lot of hired help come and go and as Harold remarked one time when one of their men announced that he was leaving, "I don't blame you. If I was a young fellow I wouldn't work for people like us, either." He knew that their lifestyle was more than a little different than most, but his loyalty to Maurice was as great as his brother's was to him.

Most housing for hired help in this part of the country wasn't that great, but often the housing of the people who hired help wasn't that great, either. Kings just didn't feel compelled to provide average or better than average housing.

Why should the hired help have better housing than the employers?

Once when Maurice was complaining about how hard it was to get good help, a neighbour said, "Well, Maurice, I guess you should have got married and raised your own."

"Maybe I should have," said Maurice, "but Joe Heaton got married and had two sons and I own his place." It was a pretty snappy comeback and a true one.

The Heaton place was an old ranch and one of the best known ones in the country, both for the fact that church services were held there before a church had been built, and for its generous hospitality. The old stone house was a landmark. It had been abandoned years before Maurice bought the place as it took too many tons of coal to heat. At one point in time, it had been converted into a furniture factory, but that venture failed, so it was just another large abandoned country house.

Several people wanted to buy it and move it and Maurice would have sold to any one of them had they been able to come up with the money. The old stone house still sits there and I'm sure Maurice thought of it as a monument to futility—why build a mansion you can't afford to heat? I'm also quite sure he enjoyed owning it.

Chapter 12

BURIALS AND OLD AGE

*H*arold Augustus (Raoul or Rold) King, was born April 10, 1899, died on June 13, 1995 at the age of 96 and was buried in Livingstone Cemetery north of Cowley where both his parents and his sister Polly, or Dolly Bell, were also interred. The Rev. Brian Wiig conducted the sermon in the little Anglican Church of St. Aidan's in the village of Cowley and Virginia Delinte, a neighbour and friend, gave the eulogy for Harold.

She was reduced to tears as she spoke. So were some of the congregation. Both men had inspired affection and respect in many of those who knew them, but it was Harold they meant when they said, "Everybody liked him."

I often thought that Maurice was hurt that people took to his brother so much more easily than they did to him. But he had learned along the way not to worry about whether people liked him or not, as long as he survived. One of the two brothers had to be suspicious, and it was Maurice who felt he was protecting his younger brother from people who might take advantage of him. I was the organist at Harold's funeral, and for prelude music, played many western, cowboy-type, sacred songs which I thought he might have liked. He might have, too, although he also liked classical and semiclassical music.

The older brother, Maurice Rupert King, was born September 17, 1898, died August 22, 1996 and was also buried in Livingstone Cemetery. Both men were born at Colchester, Essex, England. Funeral services for Maurice were also held in the little Anglican Church in Cowley, Alberta, with the Rev. Brian Wiig again officiating. Maurice also was interred at Livingstone Cemetery north of Cowley. It is a beautiful little cemetery enclosed on three sides with caragana, and with the Livingstone Range of the mountains to the west. The Canadian flag flies year round and the prairie grass waves gently in the west wind. The wild birds fly overhead and the two brothers are reunited with their parents and their sister. It is a fitting place for the King family.

Again I was the organist but this time I gave the eulogy, too. I was honoured to be asked and had a lump in my throat as I spoke of the deprivations and hardships he had suffered in his youth, and also as I thought of his last days, surrounded by people who wanted the estate it had taken him a lifetime to put together. Friends of his, Mr. and Mrs. Denver Reimer sang a duet, and Gina Hoffman, Russell John's wife, and her sister sang "Whispering Hope".

Maurice had gone into hospital a few days before he died, a sick old man who was very much alone. The last time I went into hospital to see him he was asleep and I did not wake him but stood by the bed and said a brief silent prayer and goodbye. If pity is akin to love then I had loved Maurice. He was always good to me and I had admired his honesty. I think it could be truly said of him that he did the best he could, and stayed truer to himself than most did.

In giving his eulogy, I not only told some of the facts of his early life, but I closed by quoting some lines from Poet Laureate Tennyson, who, I felt, had expressed how Maurice might have summed up his own life.

I have lived my life, and that which I have done
May He within Himself make pure! …
Pray for my soul. More things are wrought by prayer
Than this world dreams of. …
For what are men better than sheep or goats
That nourish a blind life within the brain,
If, knowing God, they lift not hands of prayer
Both for themselves and those who call them friend?

Maurice had entrusted his life, his actions, and finally, his immortal soul to the God he had loved and served.

We had been up to see him at his home a few times during his last months and Eve said we were the only ones who kept coming, that everybody else had quit. It was difficult as he was quite deaf and sometimes I wondered if he knew who we were, but at least we were company.

Sometimes he was sleeping on a low couch when we arrived and I would sit beside him and shout to ask him how he was. Often, when he had been sleeping he would take a few minutes to rouse and answer with the usual, "Well, I'm not very good, but I'm still here." Sometimes we would sit side by side on a love seat and carried on our conversation there. Mostly the conversations were repetitions of ones we had had years earlier—especially on religion, but I don't think he knew we were repeating ourselves. Sometimes I just sat beside him without saying anything, but waiting for him to wake. He often seemed to sense that someone was there and would open his eyes and have his wits about him in seconds.

We often repeated conversations from earlier years, but it was never idle chatter. I liked talking with Maurice. He had spent a lot of time thinking about the topics we discussed, and possible solutions for the problems.

One evening Eve said, "He doesn't think he's going to die. He thinks he's going to live forever." It wasn't true. During his last spring on earth, we drove up to see him. The grass was beginning to show a faint tinge of green and a few tiny flowers were scattered here and there, huddling close to the earth. Maurice was outside, a little shaky on his feet, but walking slowly. He didn't hear the truck as we approached, and I watched as he bent to the ground to pick one of the tiny buttercups and cradle it in his hands before lifting it to his face to savour its freshness. I knew that he realized that he would not have many more years to enjoy the beauty of spring.

Two or three of the last times we visited him in his home, we sat at the table and I held his old hand in mine and stroked it as we talked. He needed the human touch and I think he was beginning to feel very much like an old fox at bay, alone in the world. I wondered if he might be regretting a life devoted to accumulating material wealth while ignoring love. But I doubted it. He had learned early in life that love hurts, often doesn't last and often isn't there when you need it most. He and his brother had shared love, but now Harold was gone. And he had achieved that last wish—to outlive Harold.

As we were sitting there at his table one evening shortly before he died, he said with perfect clarity, "I made a new will this week." I said nothing and he did not add to what he had said, but I certainly wondered. I suppose I was afraid he might think we were after his money, too, and it was his, he had earned it and he could do as he wished with it. One of his executors told me that Maurice had made several new wills in the few months before he died and that he wasn't sure that Maurice knew what he was doing or what he was signing.

With the amount of money and property involved, it was

important to establish his sanity and understanding. Once he had come back to Canada from his Oregon property and announced that he had made a new will leaving everything he owned to his foreman there. His foreman here promptly got him to another lawyer where he made a new will which revoked the previous one.

I think he knew exactly what he was doing and I think that while he may have been taking the easy way, he was rather enjoying all the consternation he was causing. While he had often claimed that he didn't care what happened to his belongings after he was gone, it was not true. He cared very much and would liked to have seen the ranch continue as an entity, perhaps becoming the Canadian equivalent of the famous King Ranch in Texas. But it was not to be. The capital gains tax, so one of his executors told me, made it impossible.

Chapter 13

AUGUSTUS KING

*B*orn in England, Harold and Maurice were small children, under school age, when they sailed for North America. Their father, Augustus King had been in the textile and clothing industry in England, and may have had contracts to supply the army. But now he was looking for a change! The Boer War had ended and with it the lucrative business with the army for his products. Another rumour had it that he made his money in South Africa in ways that would not stand up to scrutiny.

But however or wherever he made it, Augustus seemed to have money when he left England. Someone has suggested they may have had woollen mills but whatever they owned, he sold his assets and was about to make a new start in a new country.

All who knew Violetta King, Maurice's mother, said she was a lovely person and many wondered why she had married Augustus. I expect she loved him. Most Englishmen of that era were expected to learn to "drink like gentlemen" and to "hold their liquor". Perhaps he did not drink a great deal when she first met and married him, but the first thing anyone who knew him here mentions is that he was seldom sober.

Often it was hard to tell at first. Andy Russell, author and mountain man, recounted hitching a ride into town from

Maycroft with Augustus, not knowing that he had drunk more than he should have. "Was that a ride!" he said, shaking his head. "I'll never forget that one. It was hair-raising."

Anyhow, Violetta and her children travelled alone across the ocean and then by train across the United States to join their father and her husband. It could not have been an easy trip but she managed.

Chapter 14

COMING TO CANADA

The move to the New World was a drastic change and the first of several moves. Augustus was an educated man and so was his wife. No one ever seemed to have taken the liberty of calling him "Gus" which was unusual in this part of the world where nicknames were the rule rather than the exception. I have never heard him referred to as anything but Mr. King or Augustus King, in spite of his drinking.

He often said that his education had not fitted him to make a living and was therefore of no use. He not only did not encourage his sons to get an education, he actively opposed it. Harold often said, "My dad taught me to work because he couldn't see that book-learning was much help in earning a living." Maurice said much the same thing and it was a sentiment that many western pioneers, having seen how useless the remittance men were, echoed. For Augustus, education apparently was not an asset.

From wherever they landed in the United States, Violetta and the children took the train to Washington State to join Augustus. They settled there only briefly. Maurice barely remembered that train trip across America but did remember the train trip from Washington when they moved to Canada. It had been spring when they left Washington, but here in Alberta, there was a raging blizzard. They stayed overnight in the American Hotel at Fort Macleod, which impressed little Maurice.

For most of his life it seemed that for Augustus the grass was always greener somewhere else. They did not stay long in Washington as he heard of the wonderful wheat crops in Alberta, Canada, so in 1906 they came by rail to Claresholm. Other moves were from one place to another in the same area, west of Granum, and the family spent the rest of their lives in this southwest corner of Alberta, moving from one farm to the next. The location of their homestead was the NE 36-11-28-W4.

While there they built a log barn and a shack that served for a few years. Orrin Hart, one of Maurice's executors, doesn't believe that Maurice's brothers went to school at all and isn't sure about Dolly. However, since both parents were well educated, they tutored the children at home and in no way could any of them be called illiterate. Their education came from the Bible and it stood them in good stead. Once when Maurice and I were talking, I said that I had never attended a university and that I had learned a lot more at home than I had at school. He agreed and said, "You learned all the important things in life from your mother." It was true.

While on the homestead, they acquired more land on Trout Creek. It was a better location with more shelter and good water. Here they built more log buildings and Harold, in particular, became really proficient in using axe and saw.

Augustus had no practical experience in farming although he was well schooled in botany and could identify most of the plants here and give their Latin names. Instead of starting small and growing as he learned, Augustus bought as much land as he could afford and then lost it. At least, that is what some of his neighbours said. A less educated man, who was prepared to work with his hands, might have survived better.

The new home was west of Granum and was either not the kind of land that would grow the bumper wheat crops of which he had heard or the temperatures were not right for cereal crops. Here in the hills there can be a wide range of temperatures from valley to valley within a few miles. It is guesswork on my part but he may have bought land which was more suitable to grazing than for farming.

Chapter 15

EDUCATION

*I*t was not an easy life and Mr. King was not suited to it. An educated man, he knew that his education was a handicap. He did not fit in. He was not a remittance man, he had paid his own way, but he was as useless in this new life as many of them were. The signs which said "No English need apply" were aimed at educated immigrants who were steeped in book-learning but did not know how to work.

His son Harold said over and over again, "My dad taught me to work because he couldn't see that book-learning was much help in making a living." To my mind, Harold was a bookish person who would have made an excellent scholar, but he appeared to feel that his father knew best. Harold never went to school and Maurice was a Grade 1 dropout after breaking a foot during his first year of school. He had started in September but had to stay home for part of the year when he couldn't walk, and he never went back.

Although Harold never went to school at all, he did learn to read and so did Maurice. They must have learned at home. Some have said their parents taught them to read, and to read from the Bible, and after having learned to read, both continued their educations as long as they lived. They both seemed to pity their father more than condemn him for his weakness, although Maurice said once that a liking for liquor was a curse. "It can ruin a man's life and his family's, too," he said. He knew.

Maurice may have resented his lack of formal schooling but was determined not to let its lack stand in his way. More than one person has said, "If only Maurice had had an education just think to what heights he might have risen." I always thought it might have been his lack of education which made him so determined to show the world that he could and would succeed. And he did. He never asked for pity, preferring to be envied rather than pitied.

As children, Maurice and Harold, and probably the others, too, picked rock from the land and piled it in windrows, long lines. It is backbreaking work, either under the hot sun or in the chill wind. Picking rock was just not hard work, it was hopeless as it was never-ending.

There was also a buffalo kill on their land, so the boys probably picked buffalo bones to sell, too. Anything to make a living. A friend of theirs, Doris (Babe) Burton, recalls picking up sandstone on one of their places which had finger indentations on it. Maurice's quick and inquiring mind made him wonder about the history of this country and its previous inhabitants.

It was not an easy childhood and often when the children did make a little money, their father would take it and spend it for drink. I think it was this early experience with his father which made Maurice careful about ever revealing exactly what he had or was worth.

A neighbour who knew them in their youth told me that Maurice and Harold, "the boys", were often harnessed ahead of the team to break the prairie sod. She thought if they had not been worked so hard, they would have stayed home longer.

Their parents had taught them to read, so I am told, probably from a Family Bible as they were both well versed in Scripture, much more so than most weekly churchgoers. They were knowledgeable men and alternated between admiration for those people they knew with more "book-learning" than they had and pity for those who had it and didn't know what to do with it. They had learned from their father that it wasn't always an asset but could be a liability.

They could both "quote Scripture" accurately and guided their lives by it as best they could. Maurice, in particular, being the more talkative of the two, loved to talk religion although Harold often put in his two cents worth or argued a point with his older brother. Maurice was sure, and I agreed with him, that if we all lived our lives according to the Ten Commandments we wouldn't need lawyers or a large police force and the world would be a nicer place.

He would often start a discussion by selecting one particular Bible verse and telling you what he thought before asking you to tell him what you thought. I'm not sure that he cared much what you thought. He had made up his mind what all those verses meant long before he ever met me but he was willing to listen. Often he would point a finger in the air and shake it for emphasis and say, "Can you show me a man who hasn't broken at least one of the Ten Commandments and maybe all of them?" I couldn't think of any just offhand who hadn't broken at least one but I wasn't naming names. I just agreed but I wondered if he were including himself. He would add to that statement almost every time, "I know I've broken some of them." I never did have enough nerve to ask him if he would care to elaborate on which ones he had broken or how often.

I think he was making the point that he was very aware of his own failings and thought other people should be, too. He knew exactly how many he had broken, even if he didn't tell. He also knew that he was no worse than the next man and maybe, in many respects, a bit better.

Somewhere along the way Harold had learned to play the piano or the piano accordion, and had a lifelong love of good music. Someone told me he played piano and another person insisted that it was piano accordion, the button variety. The latter instrument seems more plausible although many English families brought their pianos or organs with them when they emigrated. Then again, someone else told me that he played the harmonica or mouth organ. Unless someone gave him an accordion, the harmonica seems more likely. They were cheap and easy to carry.

He taught himself to read music from books. His favourite tune was "Marching Through Georgia". It is probably true that he was self-taught as they did not have money to pay for lessons and unless a teacher lived within walking distance it would have been impossible.

"Teach a man to read and you give him the whole world" is an old quotation. Once having learned to read, there was no stopping Harold. He bought or borrowed books on tanning and taxidermy and taught himself both trades. Marcel Dejax used to say, "I don't know how he does it but when he tans a deerskin the hair doesn't fall out all over the place." I knew what he meant because many tanned deer hides shed hair all over the floors.

His taxidermy work was also extensive and professional. Most of it disappeared before the estate was settled. I once asked Eve where it had gone and she said she didn't know but some other things had disappeared, too. Since they were not living on Sharples Creek the last few years of their lives, anyone who knew the place was there could have gone in and helped themselves.

Harold had also learned leather work from a book and from an old-timer, Coyote Johnson. One of the bridles he made went to Australia and brought him $300. It was of braided horsehair and leather. Since Bill Lagarde's sister was living in Australia she may been the connecting link.

We may never know who taught Harold log work but he had mastered the art of dovetailing the corners. When they bought the log house from either Green or Brown, they took it apart, marked the logs, and Harold put it back together again on Sharples Creek. "Harold was smart," said Willie Thibert, "he even made his own snowshoes."

Their older brother, Doug, left home when he was fifteen and went back to the States, leaving his two brothers and only sister to help their mother as best they could. Later their parents moved in with them and Mrs. King did the housekeeping and even washed the windows. Maurice and Harold had loved their mother dearly but in talks about her in his later years, Maurice often brought up the question of why a woman would stay with a man who wasn't good to her.

Chapter 16

RACHEL DWYER AND
EFFIE SMITH REMEMBER

His mother's life had a strong influence on his attitude towards women. Maurice had a tremendous sympathy for women trapped in bad marriages and for women raising families alone. He knew that his mother had little choice, especially here in Canada where she had no relatives, but often said that people marry with less thought than they choose a new car. He thought that women in particular, who had more to lose in a bad marriage, should make wiser choices before committing themselves. On the other hand he respected his mother for her loyalty to his father. She had made her bed and she lay in it.

Rachel Dwyer was surprised and amused when Maurice came to visit her after her husband Willard's death. They made polite conversation for a few moments before he got to the point of his call. Did she need financial help? Rachel says she most certainly did not need help but told him that she appreciated his concern and the offer.

Rachel also remembers the social worker who went to visit Kings when they decided they needed hearing aids. They were still living on Sharples Creek at the time in their original bachelor homestead house.

The social worker stopped at Dwyers, after trying to find the King place, and after trying to give her directions, Rachel gave up and said, "I'll go with you." She took off her apron and went and she still laughs at the social worker's composure. "I think she was from Lethbridge," laughed Rachel, "and she surely couldn't have seen anything like that house in all her born days, or met anyone like them in her whole life, but she never turned a hair and never made a comment. It was just all part of her day's work." I wondered if she had shaken hands with Harold and was wondering about having her hand X-rayed.

Maurice and Harold had been close neighbours to the H.B. Smiths, Rachel's parents, and had been frequent visitors there. They had even stayed with them when they first arrived in the country. Mrs. Smith always gave them a good meal and they had good visits as she was a cultured woman. Harold shared his love of music with Felix Smith.

Rachel also recalls Maurice chewing and breaking turkey bones with his teeth at their table, so as to get every bit of marrow out of the bones. In old age he had worn most of his teeth right down to the gums or lost them, but they had served him in good stead earlier. "I can still hear him cracking them," she said. "I never ever saw or heard anybody else do that."

Effie Smith's recollections of the King family help explain a number of things. Effie married Bernard Smith, Rachel Dwyer's twin brother. They were married in Manitoba and then they came west on Bernard's embarkation leave to see the family. Mrs. Smith, her mother-in-law, invited Maurice and Harold and Mr. King for dinner so they could meet and inspect the bride, "Mrs. Barney". Maurice never called Bernard anything but Barney.

This meeting was the beginning of a friendship between Effie and Augustus King. "I called him Gussie," she said. "He was a small man and extremely neat, always. He had snow-white hair and he was the only man I've ever met who never just took his hat off—he doffed it. It was the gesture of a gentleman. He was a quiet man, too."

Bernard and his family had prepared her for two long-haired, unshaven, shabbily dressed visitors, and she said she was disappointed. They looked quite normal, had haircuts and were clean shaven for the occasion and were dressed in their best clothes. Maurice even wore a leather belt. Most of the time he held his trousers up with binder or baler twine. "After dinner," said Effie, "Mr. King went into the living room, sat down at the piano, and played for us."

Mrs. King had died in 1941, a few years earlier. "The family had owned King Woollen Mills in England and Mrs. King had worked in the mills," said Effie. "His family thought he had married beneath him and would not have anything to do with her. They cut him off socially. It made him bitter towards them. But he adored his wife.

"I think he was a concert pianist. He certainly could have been. Since the Smiths had a piano and he didn't, he would come to their house to play. He would walk in, doff his hat, say 'Gud afternoon, ladies' and sit down at the piano and play for hours. He played Brahms, Beethoven and other classical composers but he could also play some of the popular music of the day. He played beautifully and when he had played for two or three hours and was finished, he would get up from the piano.

"'Well, it's about time,' Mr. Smith would say, and he and Posthole, my father-in-law, would have a couple of tots of whiskey together and he would go home. If his sons smelled the liquor on him, they figured he had been drinking all afternoon and I don't think he ever told them. He didn't want them to know how badly he missed having a piano. Sometimes he played at parties, too. He got a small remittance from England but I don't think it was very much.

"When we went back to the ranch after the war, with our first baby, they came over as soon as they heard, to inspect Barney's son. Next day Maurice was back, bringing with him his mother's wicker rocking chair. 'You can't raise a baby without a rocking chair,' he said.

"Harold came two weeks later with his gift. 'Can you sew, Mrs?' he asked me and when I said 'yes', he gave me a beautiful tanned piece of deerskin. 'You make a buckskin jacket for the baby,' he said and I did. He beaded it later and all five of our children wore it. Maurice was godfather to our son Reg. He wore clean clothes and shaved for the baptism and also for Mrs. Smith's funeral, a sign of respect."

One Christmas when they were coming to Smiths for dinner, they did not appear until nine o'clock, two hours later than expected. Everyone worried that something might have happened to them but didn't know where to start looking. When they did show up, they were stinking. They had been in a wolf den on Indian Creek. They were after the pups when the bitch returned and had them cornered. They finally managed to shove the pups out and when the mother led the pups away, they escaped and came to dinner.

Effie recalled that once when their big garden got hailed out, Maurice went out with a bucket, gathered the hailstones and made ice cream with some canned milk. Maurice drank malted milk and they also made root beer. Once the caps from their bottles all popped and the root beer leaked through the ceiling from the attic onto their heads.

Effie and all her family were good friends. "Once," she said,

"Harold hauled a thirty-two pound watermelon out of their ice house and we and our children ate the whole thing at one sitting.

"I remember one time Maurice's horse stepped in a badger hole and fell, breaking Maurice's leg. He walked five miles home and had his hired man, Jack (or John) Smith drive him to the hospital, where they not only set the leg but gave him a bath." Later Maurice came to Effie and said, "I want you to show that woman (the hired man's wife) how to look after a child. She doesn't know anything."

"One of Maurice's social skills in earlier years was checkers. He and Bernard would play checkers for hours at a time and Maurice would take as long over one checker move as he would over an important business deal. Harold used to play cribbage with my father-in-law.

"Every time we went to a rodeo we took Maurice along," she continued. "Once when Bernard and I were alone with him, he insisted on taking us to dinner at a local restaurant. He ordered steak for all three of us but when it came, he said we weren't paying for steaks that were green. He refused to pay and we all walked out. He said if we couldn't eat it, we sure weren't going to pay for it. And we didn't."

Chapter 17

A LITTLE ANTI-MARRIAGE

*T*hose of the family who had stayed in Canada stayed in close contact. Family loyalty was a virtue and they practised it. Maurice and Harold were not only close in age but were close in every way, sticking together through thick and thin until death did them part. The poverty and hardships they had shared in their childhood proved an inseparable bond between them. At the last, when Maurice wanted only one thing— to outlive his younger brother—it was because he felt that he could survive without Harold, but that Harold could not survive without him.

Marcel Dejax had said more than once that if it had not been for Maurice, he thought Harold would have married and lived a more normal life. I suspected that at times Maurice would have liked to get married but could not bring himself to desert his younger brother. He liked women and Harold was afraid that even when his brother was over seventy, that he still might marry. Maurice brought up the idea of hiring a housekeeper in their old age and Harold was violently opposed. "You do," he said, "and you'll end up marrying her. We don't need one as long as I can cook."

Chapter 18

Anti-Alcohol

Augustus King was not naturally a mean man and Maurice knew it. He simply did not have the means to support his wife and family as they should have been supported. He may have been a weak one. Someone once described him as a man out of tune with the world around him, a man who drank up what should have gone towards a decent living for his family and himself. I suppose it was an escape for him. I never once heard Maurice say an unkind word about his father, but I often heard him talk about the evils of "drink" and the harm it did to a family.

He knew first-hand of what he spoke and would never touch alcohol. Neither would Harold. Just plain water was Maurice's favourite drink although he drank green tea at times, and also fruit juice or milk and I have known him to drink a milk shake. He would have considered it a healthy drink. As Effie Smith mentioned, they had a liking for malted milk, too.

Chapter 19

EATING RIGHT

*T*heir diet was enough to make a nutritionist have nightmares. Jokingly I have said several times that if only they had eaten right, they would have lived longer. Beef, almost raw, was a favourite food although they also ate a lot of fish which Harold caught in Sharples Creek, Heath Creek, and the North Fork of the Old Man River. Trout and grayling, both fresh and canned, contributed to their diet. Harold put down food from the garden and wild fruit in quart jars for winter and Annie Dejax sometimes canned surplus fish and wild game for them. She also baked bread for them at times.

They ate butter by the pound with the baked bread, never margarine that I know of, but good store-bought dairy or creamery butter. What they bought at the store was not much. Butter and ice cream, which they ate by the gallon when they could get it, were two luxuries in later life. They had often eaten bread with no butter or bread with lard in earlier times and had hungered more than once for an ice-cream cone or a Dixie cup. Those "water for lunch" days were not soon forgotten.

One winter they lived mainly on elk, or "alk" as they called it. Wild game which Harold shot provided a lot of their food in those early times. They ate bear and moose and deer. I don't know about wolf. Harold trapped enough of them but I think one has to be desperately hungry to eat the meat. Wolves tend to be on the lean side and well muscled so that the meat is stringy and tough. The only reason they didn't get scurvy is because they had the home-canned fruits and vegetables.

The one treat Maurice had allowed himself in early years was salted peanuts. In later life he developed an allergy to nuts and could not eat anything that had nuts in it. His one treat in his old age was chocolates which he loved. He rarely shared them with anybody. "I can go for months and never eat a chocolate," he once told me, "and then I might eat a whole box at a sitting. Except the ones with nuts." I guess his body craved the sweets.

I could understand because I did the same thing myself— except that I never hoarded boxes on hand in case the craving should come on unexpectedly. He did and when he died, he had six or seven boxes of unopened chocolates. People who came to his funeral and the lunch which followed got to sample them in his memory.

I never once heard Maurice complain about lacks in his childhood but he never forgot what it was to be hungry and no one ever left their home that way if he could help it. Their hospitality was legendary, even if simple, and he felt deeply for the genuinely needy. But he knew that in many cases, if people had put first things first and done without frills, as he and Harold had done, they could have sufficed without suffering.

I don't think the King Brothers ever ate vitamin pills but in summer they did eat lots of fresh vegetables from the garden down by the creek. Harold tended that garden and it was a good one, contributing immensely to their table.

Like most farm families they had a root cellar for root vegetables and all year round ate their own potatoes, turnips, carrots, and maybe beets and parsnips and cabbage, which also kept well. With the coming of electricity and deepfreezes, root cellars have more or less gone out of style except for the huge ones used by commercial growers, but early pioneers, with no other means of preserving food raised in summer for winter use, dug holes in the ground, shored them up with timbers so they would not cave in, put a small ventilator on top for air to circulate and a door of some kind for entry. That hole in the ground, as long as the door was kept closed, would keep potatoes, beets, cabbage, turnips and carrots and other items from freezing.

They raised potatoes for sale, too. Einar Nelson, foreman for the Waldron, had hired Maurice and Harold when they first came to the country so when Maurice needed help he went to Einar Nelson to see if he could hire his son. Ronald Nelson remembers their coming to get him one spring to sprout potatoes. Their potatoes were still in the root cellar. They must have had a bumper crop the previous year because they still had a big surplus come spring. They had kept well but as potatoes do, they had sprouted and the sprouts had to be removed before they could sell them to the work crew down by the South Fork.

Maurice showed Ronald into the root cellar and then left the fourteen-year-old boy with a lantern and went out and closed the door on him. There was no way he was going to pay a boy for goofing off or clowning around and when he was shut in, Maurice knew exactly where the boy was and what he was doing.

Harold got up about two in the morning, hitched up the team and wagon and hauled the sprouted potatoes to the crew, got the money and came home with it all in his pocket.

Chapter 20

THE FREE LUNCH

I don't know what he had for lunch that day but Maurice was known for his lunches or lack of them. He would often trail cattle into the Community Auction Sale in Lundbreck in the early days. It was a two-day trip herding the animals on saddle horse. He would leave home early in the morning, long before daylight. Herding cattle in the dark was not an easy job but once you got them on a road between two fences they couldn't stray far. Often he stayed overnight at the Wildcat Ranch owned by Dewart Smith as it was a halfway mark between the two places. There he would be fed and continue on his way next day.

Lundbreck is still a small hamlet but it has almost always boasted a restaurant of sorts, and various women's church groups took turns catering at each and every sale. A church group in which I worked charged a dollar or maybe a dollar and a quarter for a full meal with home-made pie for dessert and all the coffee you could drink. Seldom if ever did Maurice buy a meal. He would watch several thousand dollars worth of his cattle being sold, wait to pick up his cheques, and ride home unfed.

Peter Demosky tells of meeting Maurice in town. "I'm going to the cafe for lunch," he said. "Why don't you come with me?"

"Because I've got mine with me," said Maurice and he pulled

it out of his pocket, a chocolate bar which probably cost a nickel at that time.

Maurice had a soft spot in his heart for Demoskys. Mike Demosky had lived for a time towards the east end of Cabin Creek and when he retired, his son Peter took over the place. Peter's health, after a ruptured appendix and peritonitis, made him decide to sell the place. When he left the country he held an auction sale. He had been farming on a shoestring and did not have a lot of really good machinery. Most of the neighbours attended the sale and so did Maurice who bid on almost everything and bought almost everything. Peter left and the machinery that Maurice had bought stayed there until it rusted into oblivion. Maurice hadn't hauled it home. He didn't need it but he had boosted the price a little so that Peter went away with some money in his pocket. It was Maurice's way of doing a kindness.

Lunch with Maurice became a local joke although once or twice when we took him to a Waldron meeting or something similar, he not only came into the cafe for lunch but he actually paid for ours, along with his. I'm not sure just what the difference was, but another neighbour tells of stopping at Claresholm on the way to a Waldron meeting. He announced that they, he and his wife, were going into the cafe to have lunch. "I'll stay here in the truck," said Maurice.

"We insisted," said Bev, but he refused. "I felt awful, going in to eat and leaving the poor old man sitting out there alone, but he wouldn't come." Maybe he had a chocolate bar in his pocket.

Kurt Froese tells of the time he and Maurice were the only patrons in Pincher Creek's new cafeteria. Cafeteria style dining was new to the town and Maurice sat down at a table and waited for service. He waited quite a while before the owner's wife came up to explain to him this newfangled notion. She got to the end of

Maurice King finishing a meal at home in 1973.

her spiel by explaining that after he had put the food he wanted on his tray and paid for the food, he would have to carry his tray to his table before he could eat. Maurice listened carefully to every word, then got up in silence, put on his cap and left.

Chapter 21

MOSTLY MAURICE

oth of the King Brothers had good table manners. I should know as they ate at our place any number of times and we ate at theirs. Once when we were standing on the sidewalk in Pincher Creek, my stepfather from Florida nudged me and said, "Take at look at that old geezer." I did, and it was Maurice. Before I could say, "He's a friend of ours," Maurice had approached and asked Bob if he could have a ride home with us. Bob said he could and to my stepfather's surprise he found himself sharing the back seat of the car with "that old geezer".

When we got to our place, he came in for lunch with us and I whipped up a shrimp creole. Maurice had two or three servings and then spent the better part of the afternoon with us before our oldest son drove him home and returned with a packet of green tea Maurice had given him as a thank you.

In the last few years of his life, on his car or bus trips to his Oregon ranch, he either properly brown-bagged it with a lunch put up by Eve Hoffman, or went into the bus depot lunch counter. "I was always the last one to be waited on," he once said to me. I didn't have the heart to tell him that he just didn't look like the last of the big-time spenders. Those lunch counter waitresses can size up in a jiffy who might tip and who won't. Maurice just didn't look like a non-tipper; he looked like he might not have enough cash to pay for a coffee.

Once, on one of his trips, so he told us, he was counting out some cash carefully, when a stranger asked him if he wanted help, that he would give him a couple of dollars. "I'm not broke," replied Maurice. "I own a few ranches, but thank you very much for the offer." He was amused at this incident knowing that he was worth more than all the people on the bus put together. He often got pleasure from that knowledge, knowing that people were judging him by his outward appearance while he knew that he could buy and sell them a hundred times over.

As mentioned earlier, when they first came over the ridge they lived under tarpaulins or in barns. Mrs. H.B. Smith had them live with her family for a while and he never forgot her kindness. She was English born and an educated woman and he enjoyed talking with her, although there were times when she, a busy woman, wished he would go home and leave her to her work.

Eventually Kings bought the Sharples Creek quarter where they were to spend most of their lives. Sharples Creek was named after the first settler on it, a man who came with some horses and then left. They had few neighbours, but were good neighbours to those they did have, although Maurice always referred to Green and Brown who lived two houses up the creek from them as "the coloured folk". It was his idea of humour.

I believe one of them owned the two-storey log house which Maurice and Harold later called home. It must have been a nice house originally. "I went into the bank," said Maurice, "with five dollars in my pocket, and asked for a loan. I don't know why the manager gave it to me, but he did. We had a reputation for honesty and thrift and for hard work, and maybe he had heard of us. Anyway, he gave us the loan which got us started."

While I hesitate to use the word "grovel", in all the years I knew Maurice and Harold, bank managers almost fell over themselves trying to get their business. Maurice was then the only person I knew who had a special arrangement so he could get into the bank after hours. Our bank in Pincher Creek, the Royal Bank, even had birthday parties for him complete with cakes. He was worth a fortune to them. He loved the special attention. After the early years of poverty, that, in itself, was a reward. It amused him, too, to know what attention money could bring. "You got one dollar in your pocket," he was fond of saying, "and you got one friend. You got two dollars, you got two friends."

When he was a year or two past ninety, he was still wheeling and dealing. "Maurice wasn't really a good cattleman," said Warren, one of my own sons, "but he was hard to beat as a businessman." Anyhow, at over ninety, he was negotiating for another ranch and was annoyed and surprised when the manager said firmly that it would have to be over a ten year repayment period, not twenty-five, as Maurice had requested. He got the loan and I'm quite sure he repaid it within the specified time. He would have had water for lunch three times a day before he reneged on a debt. However, it was true that he seemed quite sure he would live forever.

"He thinks he's never going to die," said Eve. Since Maurice's determination was one of his strongest characteristics, I thought he might not. I knew with one part of my mind that he would, but knowing Maurice as I did, I wondered.

Wheeling and dealing kept Maurice going. He enjoyed doing the math in his head, the math necessary to figure out the interest on the principal over a given period of time, calculating the price of a herd of cattle at so much a pound and trying to figure out whether he was making any money, just breaking even, or losing. I rarely saw him use a pencil and paper—he was an expert at mental arithmetic.

Chapter 22

MAURICE AND WOMEN

*P*eople sometimes referred to Maurice and Harold as hermits. A hermit is a recluse who has retired from society. They were definitely not hermits. They may have lived in a remote area but they went out to social gatherings and accepted dinner invitations. They also entertained a lot of company in their own home, but on a casual basis. They both liked people, even if they didn't trust them very far.

Maurice told me once that women thought he was a social failure. That may be. I liked him but in a purely platonic way. I knew a number of other women who also liked him. He said that he only ever went to one dance and when he asked a girl to dance, he stepped all over her feet and she told him what she thought of his clumsy ways and walked off the floor and left him standing there. That ended his dancing days.

"There was only one woman I ever wanted to marry," he said once, "and she didn't want to marry me." I hadn't a clue who the woman was but someone later told me that he was sweet on Margaret Kemmis so she might have been the one. She married Pat Kelly, an Irishman known for his long legs. "It would keep a person busy all day just packing water to wash Pat Kelly's long johns" was a local saying. He was a long drink of water, only unfortunately for everyone, he usually drank liquids much stronger than water.

Once he arrived at a local ranch so drunk that when he got off his horse in the barn he fell on the ground and couldn't get up. He just lay there, dead drunk. "We all kept Margaret from seeing him," said Norah Porter, "but maybe we would have done her more of a favour to make sure she did. Nobody thought she should marry him but I guess it is true that love is blind."

"I saw her some time after she got married," Maurice said. "She was wearing an old dress and was down on her knees scrubbing the floor. She had two or three small children. And I couldn't help but think that she'd have been better off to have married me. At least, I'd have been good to her." He would have, too.

A local man tells me that the woman Maurice wanted to marry was an attractive woman half his age. It was becoming obvious that she needed a husband. She refused him. Someone else later told me the same story.

A woman from Claresholm, who is a grandmother now, perhaps even a great grandmother, told me that Maurice once came courting her. She was working for her uncle at the time and the uncle, as he did with all her suitors, put a fast stop to the courtship. "I was working cheap for my uncle," said the woman, "and he didn't want to lose me."

Maurice was fond of another Margaret, Margaret Smith, his Oregon foreman's wife. He had known Margaret and Johnny when they worked for the Waldron Ranch and trusted them to manage his American Ranch. This other Margaret had taken up oil painting in her middle age and presented him with one or two large framed landscapes she had done. They hung in the kitchen of their home on Sharples Creek and Maurice seemed quite proud of them. He thought she had real talent. Once he asked me what I thought of the pictures and I gave a noncommittal answer. They were pretty enough but not, in my opinion, exceptional in any way.

Later Belle Cote, an artist in her own right, mentioned the pictures. "She's not a real artist," Belle said. "She just copies." I had to agree. She was an excellent copyist but not a real artist. However, Maurice loved the pictures and that was the main thing. He was convinced that Margaret was an unrecognized genius.

Chapter 23

COMPANY FOR DINNER

*P*eggy Robbins must have impressed Maurice as a lady. Peggy had taught in a one-room school named Tanner, north of Cowley. There she met and later married Peter Demosky. Maurice met Peter in town one day and said, "I hear you got married." Peter said he had. "Well," said Maurice, "bring the missis up to dinner on Sunday." I don't believe they often invited people to dinner although they fed a lot of people who just dropped in. Peter said he would, and come Sunday, he and the "missis" (a common appellation then for a married woman) drove to the King Brothers' home for dinner. The table was not only cleared, it was set with a white cloth. "We had a really good dinner," recalled Peter. "I think we had fried chicken (home-grown) and lots of potatoes and vegetables which were also home-grown. When we had finished all that, Maurice got up and went around the table to where Peggy was sitting and said, 'Now, missis, what would you like for dessert?'

"'Well,' said Peggy. 'What do you have?' Maurice listed half a dozen things also mostly all home-grown, or hand-picked, canned raspberries, canned wild strawberries, canned saskatoons, canned gooseberries and one or two home-canned store-bought fruits like peaches or pears. I forget what she chose but they cleared away

Harold King finishing a meal at home on the King Ranch in 1973.

the plates and served it nicely. Harold had put all those things up in quart jars during the summer. It was a memorable occasion."

It also proved that Kings knew how things should be done and would do them for the right company, the right company being invited guests whom they liked and respected, not people who just happened along.

Chapter 24

THE CIRCUS

One incident Maurice told me about several times was the day they went to the circus. It broke my heart, although it may not have been much of a circus at that time. The circus was coming to town and Mr. and Mrs. King decided that the children should see it so off they went, the children in the buckboard harnessed to the team.

I don't know which child clutched the quarter, but when they got to the circus they learned that admission was not a nickel each but a dime, and the quarter would not get them all in. They discussed whether the two younger children should go while the others waited for them and finally decided that none of them would go.

Instead they bought a book which they could all enjoy and went home. "I don't remember the name of that book," said Maurice, "but I know we read it over and over again until it fell apart and the pages got lost."

For the rest of his life he regretted the circus he had never seen. When he was in his nineties I invited him to go to the Shrine Circus in Lethbridge with me. He had always said he would have liked to have seen an elephant. But by then he was almost completely blind and he refused. I was annoyed. Perhaps he felt he would

Maurice King at home on the King Ranch.

not enjoy it, or perhaps he felt that circuses are for children, and perhaps he was right, but I went alone and I enjoyed it. I wished he had come with me, and I still wish he had come.

Chapter 25

DOLLY

One other woman in Maurice's life was his sister Dolly. Maurice called her Polly, but Maurice had a habit of calling people by names other than the ones most people called them. He was fond of Dolly and several times when we were going to Calgary for the day, we would phone and offer him a ride. He always accepted and we dropped him at her comfortable North Calgary home and then picked him up later. He never once volunteered any information about what kind of a visit or a day they had had.

Dolly was a girl Matthew Halton was not apt to forget. Matthew Halton, later a nationally known CBC commentator, taught school at Heath Creek, north of Cowley and not far from where Maurice and Harold lived. Once, Halton visited the Sunday School held in the schoolhouse and made a point of talking to each boy and girl present. He made a special point of asking each child's name and would then mention that he knew their parents or other family members. All went well until he came to Dolly, who was hanging back to one side, chewing a straw.

"Whose little girl are you?" asked Halton and Dolly answered, "Huh!" Matthew may have been taken aback but he was not daunted. "You know me," he said. "You saw me yesterday."

"I never saw you before in my life," snorted Dolly.

"Yes, you did," said Halton.

"Where?" Dolly asked. "Where did I see you?"

"I waved at you yesterday," said Halton. "I was riding that white horse across the coulee from here."

"Was that you?" Dolly asked in surprise.

"Yes, it was," said Halton, "and I waved at you. Don't you remember?"

"Shucks," she said. "I remember, but I thought it was a sack of potatoes tied in the middle."

Dolly was as tough as her brothers in some ways but she knew there was a better way to live than the way they did. Once when she was visiting them, somebody dropped a match which fell through the cracks of the board floor.

"Somebody better find that," warned Harold. "Mouse might start a fire with it."

"Good thing if it did," said Dolly. "Might burn the place down." I'm sure a match dropped on the floor of Dolly's home would not have fallen through a crack.

Once when she thought one of her brothers was being rude, she asked abruptly, "Don't you have any manners?"

"Nope," said Harold. "Don't! And can't use what you don't have."

If Dolly had startled Matthew Halton, she shocked some of the good ladies of Cowley even more. Mrs. Christie ran a small general grocery store in the village. She was not known for her gracious greetings. Mrs. Christie would slap both hands down on the counter as a customer approached, look them square in the eye and say, "And what do you want?" It was intimidating.

But the store was also a meeting place and one Sunday morning there were four very important ladies standing in the store, all in their Sunday finery, dressed for church. They all watched Dolly enter the store and approach the counter. Mrs. Christie slapped her hands on the counter and gave her usual "And what do you want?"

"You got anything to drink in this joint?" Dolly said clearly. "I'm so goddamn dry I could spit dust." None of the ladies fainted but they talked about it for days.

Dolly was good on a horse, better than her brothers. At Pincher Creek rodeos, she could trot alongside her horse with her hands on its withers and then suddenly leap over it onto the other side and back again. "She was well built," said an admirer of hers. "She must have been five foot ten or so."

As a small child, Rosella Thibert recalls walking home from Heath Creek School one day when Dolly King rode up beside her and said, "Gotta match, kid?"

Rosella said, "Why would I have a match? My father would skin me for carrying matches."

Years later, Rosella said, "She must have known I wouldn't have a match, but she had this hand-rolled cigarette dangling from her mouth and nothing to light it with. I was scared of her."

Another person who remembered Dolly well was Doris Burton. Doris was the daughter of well-known guide and outfitter Bert Rigall. She married Ed Burton and they went to live in the Gap in the Livingstone Mountains where Ed was hired by the North Fork Stock Association to herd cattle on the Forestry allotment. The Stock Association provided a log cabin for their rider, and Doris and Ed made their home in that.

Not long after they had set up housekeeping there, the King Brothers and Dolly arrived to visit them. Doris was a very petite, pretty girl and Dolly looked her over carefully and then said to

Ed, "Don't know why you'd want to go and marry an ugly little thing like her? I bet you wanted her father's money."

She didn't say, "When you could have had me," but Doris suspected that Dolly might have had an eye on Ed herself. He had taken her to a dance or two and when dressed up, Dolly was an eyeful.

"I knew she did it to hurt me," said Doris, and it did, "but the part that hurt most was that Ed didn't say anything."

"Did your dad have money?" I asked when she told me the story years after it happened.

"No," said Doris, "but he ran a good outfit so it might have looked to people like he did. But he was always borrowing at the bank."

Dolly later married a ranger by the name of Jack Bell. He was a Forestry man and Dolly was strict with Forestry people. "She charged them for meals," said one man. "It might have been Forestry policy that their rangers not be out money for meals. I do not know."

I would liked to have met Dolly but in all the times we drove Maurice to her home in Calgary, we were never invited in.

Chapter 26

THE COURTING SUIT

I never heard of Harold's being seriously interested in a member of the opposite sex. But one story has it that he once bought a suit to go courting. Then he lost his nerve and left the suit in the box in which it had come. When his mother died he decided he would wear the suit to her funeral but when he opened the box, the moths, or the mice, or both, had eaten all the cloth and there was nothing left but the buckram and the buttons.

In all the funerals I saw them attend, either as pallbearers or mourners, they always wore their flannel shirts and blue jeans. Maurice, being on the short side, usually had his pant legs rolled up, sometimes to the tops of his gumboots. The blue jeans might be held up with baler or binder twine but they were clean, or at least cleaner than his regular everyday working jeans.

They attended a lot of funerals as honorary or active pallbearers. Appearances were not that important to them and they had dressed as best they could.

Chapter 27

MORE THOUGHTS ON MARRIAGE

Maurice had a lot of thoughts on marriage. Harold may have had some, too, but he was less vocal than his older brother. Maurice took marriage very seriously and thought other people should do so, too. He may have read it somewhere or heard it from someone else but I'm sure I heard it from him that a man spends more time and care choosing a car than he does a wife. If that is the case, then it is no wonder that some wives don't last as long as some cars.

Maurice was fond of comparing a wife to a man's left hand, a Biblical allusion. That meant that the husband was represented by the right hand. "Now," he would say almost accusingly, "if the right hand doesn't know what the left hand is doing, how can they get along? How can they work together?" I don't think he expected an answer; he just liked to think he had people stumped. And most of the time he did. When I replied that lots of women didn't have a clue as to what their husbands were up to a lot of the time, he grinned and said he guessed it was true. But he recognized more than most men of his time that marriage was, or should be, a partnership of equals.

He and Harold both spent a lot of time talking to Doris Burton's husband trying to make him see that he should be better to her than he was. They had a Christian philosophy as regards marriage and women. It may be, that having seen their mother suffer, they wanted to help other women avoid that fate. And, as Doris wrote in her book, *Sunshine, I Made My Own*, for a time it seemed that they had succeeded. Her husband improved to the point where she said she had the kind of marriage for a few years that she had always dreamed of having.

Chapter 28

WOLVES

Their older brother had left home as soon as he was old enough but when Maurice and Harold decided to leave, too, it was not for the States. When they first came to the Porcupine Hills as boys, somebody had given them traps and so they became wolfers, men who trapped wolves. In the late twenties, an adult female wolf pelt would bring between $100 and $150 and a pup pelt was good for another thirty, a fortune to the two boys. But they also trapped the animals alive and sold some of them to the zoo.

Saving the wolf from extinction was not a national priority then. Later when environmentalists espoused the cause of the wolf, Harold made headlines in the *Lethbridge Herald*. Something was attacking their cattle that winter and had killed a calf or two. Protecting one's livestock is a priority with most ranchers and Harold was a better shot than most. He was also an excellent tracker and knew from the tracks in the snow that a pack of wolves was harassing the herd.

For several mornings in a row, he got up in the dark, snowshoed out to the feed ground where the cattle were and staked himself out where he could see them. He got there well before daylight and lay there in the dark and the cold until the wolves appeared.

He was not a young man but he was a determined one. He kept up his vigil until he got one or two of the wolves and scared the other ones away.

Unfortunately, someone he mentioned it to either leaked the story to the newspaper or told someone who did. There was a temporary outcry against cruelty to animals, but Harold defended his actions with the plea that he had killed the wolves cleanly and quickly, not slowly and in agony like the calves they had killed.

Chapter 29

THE BEAR FACTS

Harold's hunting ability was legendary. For a number of years they had made their living by trapping. One story has it that Harold went into a bear's cave with a revolver, a flashlight and a snare, to get the sleeping bear. Once in there with the bear, he found he didn't have enough hands, so he crawled back to the entrance and gave the revolver to Maurice. As he turned and crawled back into the cave, Maurice remarked that Harold's heart was in good shape because he could hear it pounding. Harold replied, "That ain't my heart. That's the bear's heart you can hear."

There is a somewhat similar true story about Maurice. Once, he was in a discussion about bears and their hibernation habits. The conversation resulted in a wager. No money changed hands but the loser would owe the winner a week's work. "I'll bet," said Maurice, "that I can go into a hibernating bear's den and put a rope on him. You hold the other end of the rope and haul him out if you want." Maurice crawled into the den and put the rope around the sleeping bear's neck and then crawled out and handed the other end of the rope to the other fellow. Harold, who was a crack shot, was standing by with his rifle, just in case. Maurice won the bet, a week's work.

Harold King with animals for taxidermy. He was an expert trapper.

Maurice would have loved that. He had always given a fair day's work for a fair day's pay and expected the same in return, or better.

Chapter 30

COMMON SENSE

Another story which we know to be true was related to everyday work. Southern Alberta is famous for its chinooks but they don't always last long, sometimes no more than an hour or so. A man who sets out to work during a chinook has to be prepared for the melting snow to turn to ice as the warm air disappears.

Maurice knew about chinooks and how unreliable they can be so when he set out in a chinook, he carried extra clothing with him. This particular day it was a set of long underwear. The chinook quit and Maurice tied the team to the fence and disappeared behind a haystack, where he stripped to the buff, put on his long johns and redressed so that he was suitably clad for this new weather.

One of the men who was with him said, "I couldn't believe it. The temperature must have dropped thirty degrees in a matter of minutes, and there was Maurice, as naked as the day he was born, putting on his Stanfields." It would have been only common sense to him, but then he knew that common sense was often pretty rare.

Chapter 31

AUCTIONS

hatever they lacked, it was not initiative and ambition. They would work at anything, and they did. They were honest and they lived frugally. They bought one quarter section from a homesteader who was giving up and moving out.

He held an auction when he moved and two people showed up, Harold and Maurice King. Chances are the homesteader didn't have much of real value to sell, but Maurice and Harold bid each other up on every item and bought everything there was. The two men were generous, particularly with people going through hard times, but they were generous in proportion to what they had. There were no frills for them and they couldn't see that other people needed them, either. They wanted to help people who needed and deserved help. Maurice believed the old saying that the Lord helps those who help themselves, but once when I told him that the saying had changed to "The Lord helps those who help themselves, but the government helps the rest," he scratched his head and said, "I believe you're right and the government seems to be doing a better job of it than the Lord."

He decried the fact that the government help went to those he didn't feel deserved it, and that the money came from taxes paid by hard-working, honest people. People like him. He didn't think it was fair.

After the first edition of this book was printed, Dr. Clarence Smith, to whom it was dedicated, phoned to discuss the above paragraph. "I know how he felt," said Clarence, "but I've worked with a lot of people on welfare and they don't have the education or the skills to get decent paying jobs. I think he was wrong there."

I did not argue the point but the King Brothers had worked at jobs nobody else would have done, and for low wages, and it was because of that Maurice begrudged tax money spent to help those he regarded as unworthy. In 1929 Harold trapped and shot coyotes, got maybe sixty or seventy, and since they were a good price, made more from them than they did from their cattle. "You couldn't beat him," said a neighbour who had known them well. "He was a crack shot and a better trapper than anybody I ever knew."

The Waldron, one of the biggest ranches in the country, gave them hunting rights and Harold stayed at the Ranger's house and shot a few coyotes from the windowsill, using fox meat horses for bait. They went fifty-fifty on those pelts and it helped. "Our grub bill one of those years was $45," said Maurice. When I stop to think that it's less than a dollar a week and that they didn't drink tea or coffee, I wonder if most of it was for cigarette papers and tobacco for Harold. Maurice would not have begrudged them for his brother.

Chapter 32

SHARING

Maurice's cheques were good. So was Maurice's word. He often said that a man's handshake should be enough to seal a deal without having a lot of lawyers involved in it. Several people have made that comment, that if Maurice gave you his word on something it was as good or better than a signed and sealed document with a dozen witnesses.

"If Maurice told me something was true," said Peter Demosky early in 2000, "no matter how wild or far-fetched the story sounded, I would believe it. You could take his word for anything." I felt the same way, although some people doubted Maurice's motives, claiming that every time he helped someone else, he managed to help himself, too.

I suspect the latter was true in the case of share cattle. At one point in his life, Maurice had share cattle on half or more of the ranches in the country. Things were tough for the ranchers and if they had to sell down their herds to pay taxes and bills, Maurice would approach them with an offer of share cattle. By that, he meant that he would put his cattle on their land, they would pasture them for him and in the spring when the calf crop came, they would get sixty percent and he would get forty per cent of the new calves. A lot of share agreements were one third to two-thirds but Maurice insisted on a sixty-forty split. In general it was a better deal for the owner of the cattle, who got one-third, than for the man who was keeping them, who got two-thirds, as the owner had no expenses. There was a little skullduggery at times but Maurice would just scratch his head and say to me, "Funny how it's always one of my calves that died. Don't know how they could tell."

He knew that the calf hadn't died at all, it just got branded with their brand, but he was content to let the matter drop as long as they didn't push it too far. Most of the people who were running share cattle for Maurice were grateful to him. He may have been making money on them, but he was helping keep them afloat at the same time. He may have helped himself while he was helping others, but the fact remains that he helped people the bank wouldn't touch.

Actually, in spite of the odd dead live calf, it was a cheap way of getting rich. He had no expenses. Maurice also had no illusions about owning land. "Some people think you must be really rich if you own lots of land," he said once, "but I might not be doing anybody a favour by leaving them land. The government could tax it out from under them." Harold agreed in this case.

It was not unusual for Harold to interrupt one of Maurice's dissertations and have Maurice retreat into glum silence for a moment or two before he changed the subject. When Harold spoke, Maurice listened even if he didn't agree. They seldom had a lengthy argument because one of them would retreat into silence until the other one began a new conversation about something entirely different.

Chapter 33

WORK

*S*hortly after they arrived on the west side of the ridge, they started putting up hay for the Waldron, working with horse teams. Where did they get the horses? "Somebody loaned them one or two and they ran them on the Forestry for free when they weren't working them. They hunted cougars on the ranch and around, too," said Bill Lagarde. "Sometimes people gave them horses to break and they worked those horses while they was breaking them. Sometimes they got up at 2 a.m. to catch the horses and harness them for work. Work was the only thing they knew."

"When they put up hay for the Waldron," said Fred Hewitt, "they took cattle in payment. That's how they got the start of a herd. They kept the wolves away from the Waldron cattle, too. It wasn't no easy job because the cattle were all over the place, but they got paid for it so they did the job."

One year they ate elk, which they called "alk", all winter. Later they raised their own pigs for meat and once made the hired man kill one with an axe, not wanting the expense of a bullet, but then they gave away the liver, parsimony mixed with generosity.

Chapter 34

ALICE

Once Maurice bought a motor from a widow in Cowley, Alice Clinton. She was a hardworking woman with several small children to support. Alice told him outright that she didn't know whether the motor worked or not but that he could have it for twenty-five dollars. He gave her the money and took the motor home.

The following week he came back and gave her another twenty-five. The motor worked but it was her honesty which impressed him and that's why he gave her the second twenty-five.

It was typical of Maurice to be generous with those whom he felt were trying. He admired and respected Alice, a woman who was doing a man's work to keep her family together.

Chapter 35

HOUSING

*M*ore than once Maurice told me about the time he went in to talk to the bank manager about a loan to buy land. He had five dollars cash to his name, but he got the loan. They became landowners, something very important to both of them. Over the years they bought more and more land, buying neighbours out and borrowing money from the bank on the strength of their names. They were hard workers and honest and responsible. I do not know whether any of their titles were joint, but I do know that they each owned land separately in their own names for tax purposes.

The one time I saw Maurice really annoyed with his brother was when Harold refused to have his land used as security for a loan Maurice wanted to buy more land. Their father had lost his land and perhaps Harold was afraid that Maurice was overreaching himself. On the other hand perhaps he was just asserting his own independence. But Harold never forgot that bank manager who gave them a start, either.

It got so that every time a place came up for sale, everyone assumed that Maurice would buy it. Usually he did, and shrewdly, he often paid less than the seller was asking. One young man was bitter.

"Maurice wouldn't go any higher than $55 an acre. He knew our place was worth more but he knew we needed the money and he knew there weren't many people prepared to outbid him. We finally sold to him for $55, and ten years later, he resold for more than a hundred."

Some people resented the fact that Maurice King was buying up so many places. One widow was determined that he would not get the place her husband had left to her. The Crown brand went with the place and the arbitrary brand in the shape of a crown seemed like a natural for the King Ranch. Maurice was determined to have it. Mrs. Wildigg refused all his offers and eventually he got someone else to act as his agent and bought it from her and got the deal signed before she knew who had bought it. Later, the house on that place, where his hired help lived, burned down, but by that time he owned more ranches with nice homes so he just moved them to another of his houses.

Some of those houses were on the Heaton Ranch, one of the most prestigious ranches in the country, and a number of people were sorry to see Maurice get that nice piece of property. Maurice told someone he didn't trust those people who had the fire, but it wasn't an insult because he didn't trust anybody else, either.

Housing was a problem. Maurice never could see why his hired men should have a better house than he did or why they should expect him to furnish one for them. So for as long as he could, he didn't. It wasn't always convenient to have his right-hand man living several miles away but it was cheaper than buying them a decent home closer to them.

Chapter 36

THE NEW HOUSE

*N*ot too many years after their mother had come to live with them and then died at their home, Harold had built a new house. It took time and he built it of logs, doing all the work himself. "I wish I knew where he learned his log work," said one man who had known them for most of their lives. "He was a real professional, an expert with an axe, but I don't know whether anybody taught him or whether he just learned." No one will ever know now. He also invented and made a home-made log peeler which the Pincher Creek Museum had on display one summer and which may be in the Claresholm Museum now. He may have used it on the logs of his trophy house, but the house in which they lived had unpeeled logs with the bark still on in places.

With their permission, Marcel Dejax showed me the new house and I admired the beautiful log interior while it was still empty and envisioned the two men settled comfortably in there. They never did move. Little by little, piece by piece, Harold's taxidermy filled the new house and it became known as Harold's Trophy House. The last time I was ever in it I admired the squirrel, the beaver, the wolf, the bear, and the elk and deer whose stuffed forms inhabited the house in which the brothers had never lived.

I thought it a pity but perhaps it was just too much trouble to move.

Eventually, in fear of losing a dependable man and his wife, Maurice bought a Waldron ranch house where their rider had once lived. They moved it to a new location on their land and added to it so that it became a comfortable home. Eve had a beautiful garden there and in their last years, Maurice and Harold reaped the benefits of having provided their help with a decent home. They moved in with Russell and Eve Hoffman and Eve cared for them like family. Every time I saw them in those last years, they still reminded me of two old alley cats who had somehow come in out of the cold and weren't sure how it happened or how long it would last.

Eve was a born homemaker, a good cook as well as good with her chickens and the flock of wild turkeys they were feeding, and an excellent, although unlicensed, nurse. The two old brothers had lit on their feet and they thoroughly enjoyed a warm house, three good meals a day, laundry privileges and towards the last, often when we arrived to visit, we found Maurice with his head almost glued to the TV screen so he could hear.

Chapter 37

BIRTHDAYS AND OTHER THINGS

We had Harold King's eighty-first birthday party at our house. I didn't think he had changed much during the two decades before that birthday, and I don't think he changed much after that, except that he eventually lost his will to live. He seemed genuinely pleased with the dinner and that we sang "Happy Birthday" to him as he blew out the candles.

Later, Eve Hoffman began holding annual birthday parties for both Harold and Maurice when they were in their last years. Many old friends and neighbours were invited and she always served a sit-down dinner to anywhere between twenty to forty guests, a meal fit for a king. The meals usually ended with two cakes, one chocolate and one white, served with ice cream which they both still loved. They didn't need help blowing out their candles, either.

Recently I met a man who had always been invited to those parties. He originally met Maurice in real estate dealings but says it was so long ago he has forgotten the details. But he does remember getting a phone call from Maurice when he and his wife were living in Stettler. He picked Maurice up, took him home and their unexpected guest stayed a week. When he announced his intention to catch the bus and go home, his host said he would

Harold King's 81st birthday party at our house on Cabin Creek Ranch. Mark Burles is sitting next to him as Harold finishes his strawberry shortcake.

drive him, that he would quite enjoy the trip himself. He made a short side trip so Maurice could see how some of his cattle out on lease were doing and then they went to either Cowley or Lundbreck. Maurice went into the store and came out with a couple of large bags of bananas and other fruit and things and said, "Here, take these home for your children." The sales slip in the bottom of the bag said $68.00. Maurice could be either exceptionally cheap or exceptionally generous, as the spirit moved him.

He could be generous or miserly as the spirit and the mood of the moment struck him. That was Maurice. If he thought you expected to get anything from him for nothing, he would clam up tighter than a clam. His was the decision as to what he would give and to whom he would give and he would keep control. He was not going to be taken if he could help it.

After our house fire he had given us quite a generous cheque. I had reason to be grateful and I never felt that he expected anything but gratitude in return. Maybe some people did feel they owed him whatever he asked in the way of small favours. I don't think he expected to be paid for helping his friends and he would have been insulted had they offered to pay him for kindnesses. We helped when we could, but I don't think he ever resented it if we said we were busy.

Sometimes I wondered if Maurice were testing people. He never took advantage of us but some people said he did of them. And from stories I heard, apparently he did. He got people who could ill afford it to haul for him, hay, cattle, pellets, whatever, and wouldn't pay until he was forced to. He was not alone in that respect. There are a number of wealthy people who got their wealth by taking advantage of others.

I played for both their funerals and never did get paid for either of them. I'm sure it would never have occurred to Maurice or Harold that anyone would be paid for a service such as that. They had been good churchgoers, at least as good as most in our area, and generous financial contributors, better than most, and would never have thought of paying for an organist at a funeral, especially a friend, someone they had known. I'm sure they thought that they had paid while they were alive.

Being friends with Maurice was a mixed blessing as I was to learn. He expected that his friends would be only too willing to drop whatever they were doing to help him, and without being paid. It didn't bother me as I always knew I could refuse and he never seemed offended, but then we didn't owe him anything but gratitude. I felt he would have been insulted had we offered to pay him for kindnesses. I was always grateful for his kindness.

Maurice was not a fence fixer and a lot of the people he hired didn't know one end of a post maul from the other. His neighbours, including my husband, often came home from fixing a stretch of the fence which Maurice should rightfully have fixed, because if they didn't, we'd be pasturing Maurice's cattle for him.

Maurice had mastered the art of procrastinating as far as fences were concerned and it always seemed to be his cattle who strayed onto and ate our grass, not the other way around. Our grass was better than his and those cattle knew a good thing when they saw it. He just let the fence lay until the other party got fed up with the situation and fixed his share of it, too.

When I mentioned to Ronald and Pat Nelson that there were two sides to Maurice, they both laughed and said nobody knew that better than his neighbours. He could be a puzzling man. He deplored the drop in morality and honesty. "At one time," he said, "I could have gone away for the day and left a ten dollar bill lying on the table, if I'd had a ten dollar bill, and could have come home and found it still there no matter how many people had been in and out of the house." He would always add, "I couldn't do that today." Locks were unknown to them as they were to many of the early settlers. Someone might be caught in a storm or stuck in a coulee and need shelter, so houses were left open for whoever might need to use them.

Once, after Virginia Delinte had driven him to a funeral and then back home again, he pressed something into her hand as he got out of the vehicle and said, "Here. Take this!" It was a twenty dollar bill which more than paid for the gas. But more often than not he expected and got a free ride from one of his neighbours.

It seemed like a waste of time to try to figure Maurice out because just when you thought you had him sized up, he surprised you. I think that sums him up—he was a surprising man.

Chapter 38

SEX AND THE BIBLE

Once, when I made a casual comment to Eve Hoffman about Maurice, she replied with, "He sure likes to talk about sex, doesn't he?" What could I say? In truth, he did. She also commented that he wasn't as nice as he wanted people to think he was. I already knew that. Given the hard times he had undergone, he knew he had to be tough because if people knew how much he was worth, they would try to get it away from him.

He thought that sex was the bond which held man and wife together and he was trying to find out from me how powerful that bond was. I never told him a thing, but just let him talk. He harped on homosexuality, quoting the Bible that it is a sin for man to lie on man or with man, and I wondered if he thought people might be talking and wondering about his relationship with his brother. Maybe he was just generalizing but sometimes I thought he worried about what people might think and say and was almost obsessed with the topic.

We did agree that often love had nothing to do with sex and vice versa, but he was the one who always brought up the topic. I had little to say, feeling that people's sex lives should be private.

He quoted the Bible often and I knew it was the book he

knew best. He read current magazines when his eyes were good but the Bible was the source for him.

In the last years of his life, he told me over and over again that the King James Version was the last version of the Bible that we could trust, that all others since then had been modified, changed, and didn't read the same way. I agreed, but, not wanting an argument, didn't mention that the King James Version was hardly the original text—that it had been altered and changed considerably before King James put his seal of approval on it.

After his death, Maurice's, not King James', I was reading a modern version of the Bible and got out my old King James Version to compare some verses and chapters. Maurice was right—there was considerable difference in wording and in meaning in some verses. So from the grave he is still teaching me. But the astounding part is that he knew enough of the Bible from memory to recognize changes in text when someone read it to him when he was over ninety.

Chapter 39

LOSING THE CASE

His honesty was considered unquestionable by most. As Peter Demosky said, "If Maurice told me something, no matter how far-fetched it seemed, I would believe it." I felt the same way, that his word was his bond and that a contract would be sealed by a handshake.

That is why Maurice was so disillusioned after a verbal contract went to court. He had rented some land to a man who claimed that Maurice had given him an option to buy at the end of the year. The price of land had gone up considerably during the year and Maurice said he hadn't given an option of any kind, but when the case went to court, the judge ruled against him. Maurice said that the man and his friends had perjured themselves.

One or two neighbours, while sympathetic to Maurice, were a little skeptical. "I think he has a convenient memory," said one. "I think he gave the option but there's no way he's going to sell at last year's price if he can wiggle out of it." Be that as it may, our bank manager was willing to stand up in court and swear that he had never known Maurice to lie and didn't think he was doing so now.

Losing the case made Maurice a bitter man. "I can't believe in Canadian justice any more," he would rasp. Having read *The*

Finest Judges Money Can Buy I was tempted to agree, but that was in the States and I wanted to think that Canadian judges are superior, less open to bribery and corruption. I hope I am right but after hearing Maurice say over and over again, on every visit, that he no longer had any faith in the Canadian judicial system, which he had always upheld, made me finally ask if he thought the judge might have accepted a bribe. He thought about that one a long time and then said, "He might have. I don't know."

Neither did I, but Maurice's loss of faith resulted in his telling local canvassers for the Red Cross and other charitable organizations to stay away from him—that he would not give them one red cent. He had not just lost his faith in Canadian justice; he had lost his faith in all other Canadian institutions, too. As far as I know he kept his word, too, although I think he did make at least one donation to our local church after his loss of faith.

Since his parents had come from England, I assumed he had been baptized into the Anglican Church as an infant. He never said, but he often came to special services at our little country church, usually when I phoned to invite him. He was a substantial contributor before his loss of faith and I'm sure he genuinely enjoyed the Sunday get-togethers and loved the Thanksgiving and Christmas potluck dinners after those services.

As he got older, and when we picked him up for church, I made sure he was seated and then filled a plate with all the things I thought he would like. He had a good digestion and was able to eat almost anything. I don't remember his ever leaving anything edible on his plate. Those church dinners were incredible. They rivaled anything a first-rate chef at a top hotel could produce as every woman in the congregation would go overboard to outdo what she had done the previous year. Maurice would tuck away turkey, ham, a mountain of potatoes with gravy, sweet potatoes, salads, vegetables, and still have room for pumpkin or mince pie, depending on the season. I never once heard him complain about being too full or having a bad case of indigestion, but I often heard him remark that it had been a good afternoon as we drove him home. Invariably he thanked us for taking him, but nearly always it was us who phoned him about going rather than his phoning us.

That was not unusual because even regular churchgoers at St. Martin's had a problem with shifting schedules and rarely knew for sure when services would be held. Our Thanksgiving and Christmas services depended on when Pincher Creek and Cowley were having theirs. They were bigger than our congregation and took precedence. Once in a while, if the road which led down to Sharples Creek and their house was impassable for a car, due to rain or snow, Maurice would have someone drive the truck up to the top of the hill and we would pick him up there. He liked coming to church and I'm sure it wasn't just for the free lunch. Harold hardly ever came.

Chapter 40

CORNED BEEF

Maurice liked his food and the one time I really disappointed him in that respect came after we had been discussing the cattle industry. We both agreed that it was not right that the only canned corned beef, which we both loved, came from South America. There is a lovely picture of a horned Hereford on the label and we were both into Herefords.

We both agreed that since there are a lot of canner cows and bulls right here at home, we should be establishing a corned beef industry here. So I wrote the Minister of Agriculture in Ottawa. He phoned to say he agreed, and we had a nice chat about the cattle industry. At that time the Minister was a rancher from the West so he knew the problems.

I told Maurice about the phone call and he was a little cynical. "Sure," he said. "He agreed with you, but will he or can he do anything about it?" I thought he could if he wanted to, but at that point in time, I knew lots about the producing part of the cattle industry, but very little about the meat packing end of it. I faithfully read the financial statements we got from one meat packing company and thought they had a better accountant than we did because they managed to keep afloat in spite of 0.1% profit.

"That's the secret," said Maurice. "Get a good accountant. The rich don't pay hardly any income tax, but folks like you and me do the paying."

The upshot of that whole conversation was that I bragged to Maurice and Harold that I sometimes corned my own beef and that it was pretty good. I told them to give me time to corn a chunk and I would invite them for dinner. Pride goes before a fall and it did in this case.

People usually corn the brisket which has lots of fat in it, too much for my liking. I wanted this corned beef to be extra special so I bypassed the brisket for a beautifully marbled rump roast to put in the brine. I had corned them before and they were delicious. I got a nice roast out of the freezer, but unfortunately I didn't give it time to thaw completely before putting it in the crock with the brine I had prepared. I left that rump there for the required three to four days and then phoned Maurice and put it on to boil. My mouth watered as the aroma began to drift through the house and as I prepared the cabbage and mashed potatoes.

The King Brothers arrived. I served the beautiful piece of corned beef on a platter surrounded with wedges of cooked cabbage, and Bob carved it at the table. It wasn't a complete disaster. It was edible but it certainly wasn't the corned beef it should have been. Nobody had told me, and I hadn't thought of it, but the brine wouldn't penetrate the frozen core of the roast so it was only partially corned. From the outside in!

Maurice chewed his way through his but didn't ask for seconds and didn't say one word of condemnation or praise. I was embarrassed and I thought it served me right. I shouldn't have bragged. Maurice never did mention that corned beef again and I always wondered if he thought that I thought that it was good.

Maurice encouraged me to let the politicians in Ottawa know what we ranchers thought, and what we were going through, and someone later told me that he not only phoned them at times, but Judy LaMarsh and some other cabinet ministers phoned him at times. He expressed his opinions succinctly and told it like it was.

Chapter 41

B R A N D S   A N D   E A R M A R K S

*T*here were two sides to Maurice, just as there are to most
people. Earmarking is a fact of life in ranching country. It
is often done shortly after birth and long before branding.
Branding comes usually in May while most calves are born earlier
than that in the year. So earmarking as a form of identification is
done within hours or days after the new calf's birth. Our earmark
is a notch cut on the under side of the left ear. Our cattle ran next
to Maurice's field after he bought the Dejax place.

One particular year Maurice branded before we did and
the brand was slapped on before anyone noticed that one little
dogie had our earmark. They pointed it out to Maurice but he
turned a deaf ear and just as pointedly ignored the remark. The
calf was branded and it was a done deed. And it stayed that way.
Maurice never acknowledged that he had accidentally branded a
neighbour's calf and he sold it that fall along with the others and
never did offer to recompense the rightful owner. Maybe he really
didn't hear.

Once when we drove Maurice to a Waldron meeting, he came
into the cafe with us and even paid for our lunch. Was he thinking
of that extra calf or was he just in an unusually generous mood?
One never knew. His refusal to buy lunch for people who drove

him hither and yon was legendary, but he never quibbled over this lunch. Maybe he felt that he had eaten in our home many times and saw this as his turn to treat.

When we visited them I saw them both. When they visited us on invitation I saw them both. But it is mostly Maurice of whom I write because we often saw him alone. We, among others, might give him a ride to town or home from town and several times even to Calgary to see his sister. Sometimes he came with us to church or to a Waldron meeting. Sometimes his hired help drove him wherever he needed to go, but sometimes he felt they should be home working so would hitch a ride with someone else. Someone he felt he knew well enough to phone and ask for a lift, but it was always, "If you're going." Never once did he offer to pay us to chauffeur him and we would not have accepted it.

Chapter 42

RATS AND MICE

*S*tories about them abounded, a lot of them untrue. Eve Hoffman told me they sometimes contributed to these stories themselves—like the time they had company and Maurice buttered a slice of bread and then said he was going to slice a dead mouse to put on it.

Somebody said that when a CBC reporter arrived to interview them, they opened the door of the house after they had been gone for a few hours and the rats scurried in all directions. That I believe, but they would have been pack rats, as this part of Alberta is still freed of the dreaded Norway rat.

Overnight visitors told of mice running around and over them when they were bedded down for the night. Most older homes had mice and most farm homes ran inside trap lines to try and keep the little critters under control.

In actual fact they did have a sock hung over the table, almost petrified, it had been there so long. Nobody knew why, and had it fallen it would have choked everybody in the kitchen.

Maurice quite enjoyed shocking people when he knew they thought he was more than a little odd. I think he just wanted to live up to his image and to entertain. Believe it or not, the stories I tell you here, to the best of my knowledge, are quite factual. If you knew Maurice, you will have no trouble believing them, either.

Chapter 43

FRED HEWITT'S TALE

red Hewitt, who was a Waldron cowboy in the early days, remembers meeting the King Brothers when they first came over the ridge.

"Maurice was riding a pinto with no saddle and Harold was walking behind him with four wolf hides." They met the foreman for the Waldron and Maurice asked for a job. They said they would take cattle in payment. Harold kept the wolves down and Maurice chored around doing whatever needed doing. Harold also took cattle in payment and that is how they started their herd. This is what Fred told Peter Demosky who was a neighbour of his.

A man from south of Pincher Creek also wrote about trying to keep wolves down to save the horses and cattle. They weren't talking about coyotes, but about the big gray lobos who would hamstring an animal. Wolfing was a good business and Maurice said that some winters Harold made more from wolf pelts than they made from their cattle.

They worked for the Waldron briefly, but later Maurice said that he only ever worked for wages less than a year of his life. Whether he counted working for cattle as the same thing as working for wages, or something different, is hard to

Glenbow Archives, NA-2864-24350-10

Maurice and Harold King started their herd by working for the Waldron and taking cattle in payment.

say. He put up hay for Pat Burns one summer but that would have been contract work.

Chapter 44

DRIVING AND CARS

A s far as I know, Maurice never owned a car and would have thought it stupid to run a car over the roads they had. He had a driver's licence but frankly admitted that he was not a good driver, that he felt more comfortable behind a team or on a saddle horse.

Once he drove off a grade and his passenger said rudely, "Where in hell you going?" I don't think he was really comfortable driving a car and as he got older, his cataracts were so bad that he could hardly see.

He wasn't a farmer. He raised green feed and sometimes cover crop when necessary, but after having seen his father's farming ventures come to nothing, he had decided that his future was in cattle. He was right, as our neck of the woods was part of the Palliser Triangle, which is an arid zone, suited to grassland and grazing more years than it was to growing cereal crops.

In many parts of Canada, ranching is seen as a glamorous career. Easterners have visions of riding the range all summer long and roping the dogies and singing around the campfire come evening, but in actual fact, putting up hay and fixing fence is what most ranchers do in the summer season. Fighting barbs and deer flies plus bulldogs is not glamorous or romantic.

Neither is fixing fence. Maurice seldom did. As I mentioned, he would just leave it lie until his neighbours fixed their half and his, too. If they tried to outwit Maurice, then it saved his grass at the expense of theirs. It may not have endeared him to them, but I don't think he much cared. He just acted like it had never happened.

I don't know whether anybody ever broached the subject to him or not but we always suspected that he was the one who had complained to the Forestry that our cattle got to stay on our lease longer than his cattle got to stay on his lease. The result was that the Forestry decided that our cattle should come out of our lease at the same time that his cattle came out of his lease.

I think that everybody was the loser on that one as suddenly the Forestry officials began paying a lot more attention to what was going on in the Porkies.

Chapter 45

ALMOST THERE

After returning from a trip to his Oregon ranch in his last years, he said that he had signed a new will while there, leaving everything he owned to the people down there. This was in spite of the fact that he had prosecuted a relative of theirs for forgery. The people on this side of the line hastily got him to a Canadian lawyer to make a new will here, thereby revoking the Oregon will.

During the last year of his life, he made several wills, according to one of his executors, and when we visited him, shortly before he died, he told me he had made another will just a few days earlier. I never once asked him about the contents of any of his wills. He had made the fortune and I felt that it was his to dispose of as he saw fit.

I'm sure almost everyone he knew was hoping to be remembered in his will and he was more than ever like an old fox at bay. During the last few months of his life, Eve said that we were about the only ones who still visited him. It was difficult as he was increasingly deaf.

His conversation had failed considerably. He repeated himself often and sometimes we just sat at the table saying nothing while I held his hand in mine. The callouses on the work-worn hand had all gone and it was soft now, but he seemed to need a human touch, reassurance that he was still in the land of the living and a member of the human race. At least, I thought he did.

When he went into hospital, shortly after that last visit in his home, I went to see him. He was asleep and facing the wall and I did not wake him. I simply said a brief prayer and left with tears in my eyes for a hurt and lonely old man whose life was slipping away. His life had been a long one and a hard one, but he had lived it as best he could. I wished him Godspeed to the better world which we had occasionally talked about and of which neither of us were too sure.

Towards the last I wondered if Maurice were ever sorry that he had not married and had a family. What he did have was brotherly love. It was obvious to everyone who saw them, that though they disagreed on many things, the two brothers genuinely cared about each other. They worried about each other and each called the other "The Boss", as though the other's word was the decisive one. They both seemed to think that they would and could live forever. When Maurice was over ninety and went into the bank to negotiate a twenty-five year loan, he was surprised that the banker insisted on ten.

Eve said more than once, "He thinks he's never going to die." I was beginning to wonder, too.

Chapter 46

NEVER JUDGE A BOOK BY ITS COVER

*T*heir usual garb was rolled up blue jeans (they never got the legs rehemmed, they just rolled them up to the right length, which was close to the tops of the gumboots) and lumberjack-style flannel shirts. They each had a pair of blue jeans they reserved for funerals and those looked new, at least unwashed, unfaded and the original dark blue.

The same held true for the shirts—the ones they wore to funerals looked new. Appearances did not count much for Maurice, but they did have a sense of dignity for the occasion, although the blue jeans would probably not be belted but might be held up with baler twine or braces, suspenders. I don't suppose either man owned a pair of dress shoes. Harold usually wore work-style boots. Perhaps they had learned a lesson from the fate of Harold's courting suit.

Most of the time appearances didn't seem to be important to either of the brothers. They were rich, they were famous, and they had done it their way. Nobody in our part of the country had been interviewed or photographed or written up more often than they had. The cover photo on this book was taken by Lowell Aldrich who had visited them with his aunt, Jeannette Burns, when he was in Canada. When he returned to California, this picture attracted a great deal of attention. It is a remarkable picture—you can even see the intense blue of the eyes.

The long, shaggy hair down to the shoulders was a trademark. When Bun Burles, my brother-in-law, was a small boy, he remembers seeing Harold King at St. Martin's Church. "It must have been an Easter service," said Bun. "I couldn't take my eyes off that long hair curling down on his shoulders.

"Finally I whispered to dad, 'Why is that man's hair like that?' Dad said, 'Shh! It's been a long, cold winter.' That was enough to satisfy me and I never forgot it."

I imagine that when the brothers were younger, they couldn't afford haircuts. Even at two bits for a shave and hair cut, they wouldn't have had the money or would have had it earmarked for more important things than hair. But we had a neighbour who lived halfway between our place and theirs and he spent a good many evenings or Sunday mornings cutting hair for the neighbours and I don't think he ever charged anything.

At our house, we owned a home-barbering kit and we cut each other's hair. The kit cost $12 new and we used it for many years. We would have cut their hair for them or they could have bought scissors and clippers and cut each others. I don't think it was important to them.

Once when Maurice and his current hired man came to Calgary with us, we had arranged to meet at SAIT where our second daughter was studying. Maurice hadn't had a haircut for some time and he was dressed in his usual lumberjack flannel shirt and jeans. They arrived at our daughter's apartment before we did and Heather's roommates were convinced that Maurice was Heather's father. She was mortified, although as we told her later, she might have done a lot worse than to have Maurice for a father. She insisted that the real father make an appearance so she could introduce him to her girlfriends and convince them that the mountain man who had appeared on her doorstep was only a neighbour.

One day when we were driving home, a tall, lanky stranger hailed us on the road north of our place and south of Kings. He was looking for Kings and we gave him directions. A few short years later we were in the Exhibition Pavilion at the Calgary Stampede. We were wandering from booth to booth when suddenly I called to Bob, "Look! Here's Harold and Maurice King."

And there they were, as large as life, two pastels of them side by side on the wall. And the artist was the tall, lanky stranger we had met on the road—Terry Bennett. I don't think Maurice ever refused a request to have his picture taken or painted, or for an interview. He enjoyed the fame.

Doug Leeds of Claresholm made a video of an interview with the two men, but mostly Maurice, a few years before they died. The video was the most popular entertainment at the Kootenai Brown Museum last winter. The room where it was shown was small but they crowded in all the people they could and turned others away. People are still intensely curious about what made the brothers tick. I still think it was the deprived childhood that made them so determined they would not be poor. They could make money, and they did, and they could hang onto it, spending it only to make more. The video made by Doug Leeds is for sale at the Museum in Pincher Creek and also from the producer.

George and Betty Dionne got some excellent video footage of the brothers who had been their neighbours. In addition, Suzanne Lorinczi, with The Pincher Creek Film Society, arranged an interview with Kings. It was conducted by Andrea Boissonault

*A Lloyd Knight Photo of the Three Musketeers, Maurice and Harold King
with their good friend Bill Lagarde.*

and Suzanne and filmed by Andy Mikita. That footage is also in the Museum.

The picture of Maurice and Harold with Bill Lagarde was taken by another well-known photographer, Lloyd Knight of Lethbridge. It is a beautiful, natural picture, probably taken in the 1950s. Lloyd's son Lindsay remembers going up to the King place with his father.

Chapter 47

FROM ORRIN HART

At the risk of repeating some statements, here are some comments made by one of Maurice's executors, Orrin Hart, who did not know he had been named and appointed Maurice's executor until after Maurice's death. Orrin Hart, a scholar, a rancher and an innovator, lives west of Claresholm and had known the King family since he was a child.

"Just after the turn of the century," he said, "Augustus King, who had been born in London, England, into a middle-class family, well educated, and much travelled by sea, came to Seattle, Washington, where he settled temporarily waiting for his wife and three small sons and one daughter born in 1900 to join him.

"Mr. King was from a well-to-do clothing family who produced clothes and supplies for the army. About the time they came to North America the family fortunes had deteriorated. He was a well spoken man, an authority on botany and could give botanical names for many plants, cultivated or wild. He was a story teller and entertainer, especially if he were baited with a few drinks. This was a great handicap to his future.

"They came by train to Claresholm, Alberta, and settled southwest of town on a small farm with a shack of some sort which provided shelter for a period until they could file on their own homestead, the NE 36-11-28-W4. While on the homestead, they built a log barn and built a shack that served for a few years.

"The boys became impatient picking rocks and building buildings, especially when their father was losing money trying to farm, and making some bad deals. Doug, the second son went back to Washington in 1925. Maurice and Harold took two horses, one saddle, and some coyote traps and went over the ridge some twenty miles away to stake out a claim in Happy Valley. They were keen trappers and lived by trapping coyotes, wolves, bear, cougar and beavers.

"They soon were able to buy a quarter section from a homesteader who was moving out and probably homesteaded another quarter.

"Over the years they lived very frugally, saved enough money to buy a few horses and cattle, and even during the Depression of the thirties, were able to expand their holdings, of course, at very modest prices.

"They both worked very hard, especially Harold, who kept very fit. The buildings they built from logs were masterpieces. They had hay sheds to cover many tons of hay to keep in reserve for a bad winter.

"With careful management, hard work, and wise investments, they accumulated considerable holdings of land. They owed nobody any money. They had enough money in the bank to see them through a bad winter after they had sold their marketable beef. They always paid their Forestry permits, their land taxes, their income taxes, their accountant and lawyers.

"When Harold died in 1995 and Maurice in 1996, the media took pleasure in calling them millionaires. The truth being known, they were far from that classification until they died, at which time their land was deemed sold for fair market value. Had anybody taken over the land as a gift, they could not have made a go of it, if they had to pay capital gains tax on the difference between the 1972 evaluation and the deemed fair market value. The ranch would not generate that kind of money. The winners were the Receiver General and the buyer of a beautiful piece of range land who could pay for it without borrowing at bank rates."

Orrin admired the brothers, and so did I, for their tenacity and their abilities. Orrin had in his possession a home-made log peeler which Harold had invented and made to take the bark from the logs he used for building. It was on the principle of a potato peeler and must have taken some strength to use, but Harold had the strength. The log peeler was on exhibit at the Pincher Creek Museum during the summer of 2000. It may be in the Claresholm Museum by now. Orrin Hart would know.

Chapter 48

FRIENDS

Maurice and Harold had friends in all walks of life—doctors, lawyers, ranchers, bankers, businessmen—many who felt it a privilege to call Maurice and Harold friends. Maurice knew that friends can be fickle. "Don't bank on them," he would say and I was never sure whether he was making a pun or not.

He spent his last few years in relative comfort, but often said that all he ever had in life was the food he ate and the clothes on his back. Sometimes they didn't have much in the way of food or clothing, but they managed and they survived.

During his long life, sometimes his trust was betrayed, but more often it wasn't. At one time he had owned seventeen brands, probably more than any other rancher in the country. He never bragged, to my way of thinking, but often seemed surprised himself at how much he owned.

Chapter 49

NEW YEAR'S AT OUR HOUSE

Maurice and Harold enjoyed several New Year's dinners with us. They both enjoyed good food, but I never saw Maurice crack the turkey bones with his teeth as Rachel Dwyer had seen him do. But then, by the time they had holiday meals with us, their teeth were well past their prime. Their table manners were good. Augustus and Violetta, one, or the other, or both, had schooled their sons well in the social graces.

On one occasion I thought they were better than those of their host. We had dinner at noon that year. We had been out bringing the New Year in the previous evening and didn't get home till three or four in the morning. I am not much of a drinker so I was up and about to get the turkey cooking and the rest of the meal underway. In short, I was feeling good.

Bob, on the other hand, may have overindulged the night before. He didn't get up very early, which was most unusual, didn't have anything but coffee for breakfast, which was most unusual, and when we took our places at the table and I set the great roast bird in front of him to be carved, he took one look at it, turned slightly green, and, without a word, left the table and disappeared.

Somebody carved the "turk" and we enjoyed a nice meal.

Neither Maurice nor Harold commented on their host's absence. I don't remember whether Bob reappeared before they left, or not, but I think he did.

But once, after a five o'clock New Year's dinner in our home in the late nineteen seventies, we spent the evening chatting. Harold was getting restless, that was plain to see, and eventually they announced that they would leave. He was out the door like a shot, never stopping to say thank you or bid his hostess goodbye with another of his bone-crushing handshakes. It was not like him at all. Maurice observed the courtesies and they left.

Later I was speaking with the hired man who had driven them to our place for dinner and asked if Harold were all right, that he had been acting strangely when they left and I had wondered if something he ate had disagreed with him.

He hedged a bit and then with a trace of embarrassment finally said, "He had to go to the bathroom and he had never used an indoor toilet and was afraid. That's why he left so fast."

"Good heavens," I said. "He could have just stepped outside to 'check on the weather'—that's what the men always used to do."

Later he spent several days in Calgary hospital, so someone must have showed him how to use a urinal. I'm sure he couldn't have lasted several days.

Chapter 50

TWO SIDES AGAIN

*M*aurice often hired help he knew nothing about. If they were willing to live like he lived, they could stay as long as they wanted. He did not pay top wages, but working for Maurice was an experience you were not apt to get anywhere else. Board was included but you ate as they ate. One boy of fifteen, who had run away from home, landed in at Kings and stayed for two years. There were no questions asked, but a cousin of the boy thinks Maurice let his mother know where he was and that he was safe. The boy's name was Brian but Maurice never called him anything but Jim.

It might not have been the best place in the world to work but there was always the prospect that he would stake you to a place of your own as he did for one or two of his employees. Or the prospect that he would remember you in his will. I think he played that one for all it was worth, and I think it amused him because I'm sure he knew all the time exactly what he was going to do. Most people with money, when the chips are down, will leave it to their blood relatives, their own kith and kin, and Maurice was fond of his sister's and brother's children. They visited quite regularly from as far away as Ontario and the United States.

As one of my sons said, "Anybody, who stays with Maurice

in hope of getting something, deserves nothing. They should be smarter."

Often his help did not stay long and most people felt that when he got Russell and Eve Hoffman to work for him, he was luckier than he should have been. Maurice apparently did not share those views, although he did see that they got shares in the incorporated ranch, and one of his executors told me that while they did not get the land or the house where they had lived, they did get cash equivalent. "We couldn't give them the land because capital gains would have forced them to sell it to pay," said an executor. As another person said, "Maurice might leave you something in his will if he felt like it, but anybody who stayed there indefinitely, counting on it, must have holes in their heads."

As mentioned, Maurice was a blend of generosity and parsimony. When he and Harold were living with Russell and Eve, he was with Eve in town one day when she came out of the store with a load of groceries. He eyed the numerous bags and then grunted something about how he didn't think he should have to pay to feed all her relatives who came to visit.

It was a cheap shot, as often when Eve's daughter Ava and her husband, Duane, and their small children came to visit, it was to relieve Eve and Russell for a few days so she could visit her people in Saskatchewan. Or they came for the day and they didn't eat that much.

Once Eve remarked to me that Maurice could be mean. I already knew it. "He's not as nice as he wants people to think," she said. But I already knew that, too. He was not a paragon of virtue. He took the attitude that what he had earned he need not share. Often, remembering the story of the little red hen, I sympathized with that attitude, but I also thought that if you want good help, you have to treat them right.

Chapter 51

HELL HATH NO FURY

On more than one occasion he hired some Americans who had crossed the border looking for work. One of them lived with his common-law wife in an old log house two miles from us. Marcel and Annie Dejax' home had been abandoned for some years. The man was fixing up the house and building new cupboards and they seemed to be creating a permanent home.

Then he did something to displease his woman. "Hell hath no fury like a woman scorned," so Shakespeare is thought to have said, and this time it was true. She knew he was an illegal immigrant and reported him. He was deported. Maurice even went to Edmonton to talk to the powers that be in an effort to keep a good hired man. It didn't do much good and Maurice lost his hired man and she lost her husband but thought it good riddance.

Hired men weren't that hard to get and the woman stayed on in the home so that it was not just another vacant house waiting to be vandalized. The case really puzzled Maurice. He mentioned it to me several times and each time would scratch his head as he said, "Don't understand why a woman would do a thing like that." He said this shaking his head in puzzlement, and sometimes with amusement, each and every time. Eventually I decided that it was a good thing Maurice had never married because he didn't know as much about women as he should have. I quoted Shakespeare to him but he still couldn't understand it. I think she wanted to go through a legal marriage and he didn't, so she got even.

Chapter 52

HOW MUCH CAN ONE TRUST

O
ne other young American he hired got Maurice to buy
him a place in Montana which he would manage. They
were a nice young couple but apparently not as nice as
they could have been because the last we heard they had sold the
place and disappeared with the money. The couple's best friend
here disapproved, but on the grounds that the man had been a
draft dodger which showed that he couldn't be trusted.

Maurice could be very trusting, and if the people with whom
he were dealing were unscrupulous, he wound up being a victim.
I think he judged people by himself, by how he would act, and
others were not always as trustworthy. I don't think he ever fully
comprehended the lengths to which some people would go to get
their hands on his property.

Once someone forged his name on some cheques. I have no
idea how much money was involved but he let the case go to
court and the forger go to jail. He said she was a drug addict and
he told me that he wouldn't be helping her any by letting her get
away with it.

He believed that one should suffer the consequences of one's
actions. One older man named Tom never got called anything but
"The Preacher". Tom stayed with them for a long time, along with

one or two other bachelors who needed a home for the winter. He did the cooking and housework which left both Maurice and Harold free for outside work.

When one of the younger hired men announced that he was leaving to go north, Harold said, "Can't blame you. If I was a young fellow I wouldn't work for people like us, either." Then he added, "I always wanted to go north when I was young." Again, when they had the chance they didn't take it.

Our second son was a Hudson's Bay Company store manager with a large house in the North at that time and he issued them an invitation to visit the Arctic. Maybe they thought they were too old. I offered to drive them to the airport in Calgary and see them onto the plane more than once, but they never did go. I don't think Maurice wanted to go as much as Harold did and Maurice was definitely the leader.

However, whether he got taken or not, the fact remains that Maurice often gave people a chance when no one else would. After the court case he lost, over whether he had given an option or not, he said he had lost his faith in Canadian justice. He also said he would no longer donate to any of the campaigns he had previously donated to, that they might all be crooked. Some people said that he never made a deal that didn't benefit himself, too. There was no doubt about that—for many years of his life Maurice was a businessman first and a philanthropist second.

Chapter 53

POLITICAL VIEWS

"*It* don't much matter which party we elect or which man," Maurice often said, "because even if they're honest when they go in, they don't stay that way long." This was during the years of political exposés and I had to agree that it seemed there were no honest men left, at least not in public life. Bribery and corruption were the order of the day.

Having read *Above the Law* and a book about the Mulroney years, I think I knew more of the details of many of the dirty deals than Maurice did, but they weren't important. Both of us agreed on that, just as we agreed that human nature being what it is, there wasn't much hope of things improving. "Laws are made for the lawyers," he was fond of saying. "They're not meant to help the common people and they don't." He was bitter at the government over farm prices. He felt that they were deliberately being kept low. I agreed with him, and so do many others, that Canada has a cheap food policy as far as home-grown products are concerned.

Taxes bothered Maurice. Their Spartan lifestyle was cheap. The road into their place was unimproved, even though they lived for most of their lives in what was called "The Improvement District". Maurice made a rather grim joke of that one—"Think they call it that because there's lots of room for improvement," he would say. He didn't like paying taxes but agreed that they were necessary. What he hated most was seeing tax dollars foolishly wasted. He could expound for hours on the stupidity of many government programs, and he did, as long as he could find someone to listen. Often it was me, because I thought he was smarter than most and worth listening to.

I sometimes thought his views were very naive even though they were right. We needed more honest people to go to Ottawa and Edmonton, people who had a little common sense and people who would keep a tight rein on the public purse and who would spend only for the public good. "You can't trust politicians," he was fond of saying and I would quote a well-known, rather cynical saying, "A good politician is one who, when he's bought, he stays bought." He would usually reply, "Well, I think you've got something there."

He had great hopes for the Reform party. Like most Albertans he had trusted and respected Ernest Manning, and the Manning name carried a great deal of weight with him. I, who had come from another province which joked about Alberta as the "funny money" province, had never voted Social Credit, but I thought and still think that Ernest Manning was the best politician this country has ever seen. True, there were hints of scandals and even a few scandals, but Ernest Manning kept a pretty tight rein on expenses and on his MLAs.

Maurice, Harold and I all wondered if his son, Preston, could control his party. We were overjoyed when the Reform party held Official Opposition status but, as Maurice succinctly stated, "He can't do much until he has the power. And if he's too honest, he ain't gonna get the power."

They liked Joe Clark, but more or less dismissed him as a

National leader. I think they both trusted western politicians more than they did eastern ones. All three of us felt that Clark was one of us. We felt that Clark was an honest man and a good one but not a great one. We compared him to John Diefenbaker, who had swept into power hoping to accomplish great things but who was eventually stymied by "The Bay Street Boys" at every turn. Maurice firmly believed that there was a national conspiracy to ensure that Eastern Canada keep the West dependent on them. He not only did not have a great deal of respect for politician's honesty and integrity, but he often didn't think much of their intelligence, either.

Chapter 54

ON GUN CONTROL

Gun control was a favourite topic of his and he was convinced that gun registration was just the start of a plot to take guns away from the honest people. "Only the crooks and criminals will have guns before long," he would lament. It was not an ignorant statement. As a man who had earned a living with a gun getting pelts for sale, and who had used a gun for protection from wild animals, he knew how important it was for a farmer or rancher to have a gun or guns.

"It's just the first step in taking our guns away from us," he would say. "First we have to register them and then they know what we have and next they take them away."

Maurice knew those tactics. He not only had a long memory but he was well read. It had happened in other countries and he did not want to see it happen here.

Even gun laws designed to protect children, such as keeping guns in locked cabinets and ammunition in a separate place, bothered him. I'm sure it wasn't personal—they weren't afraid of being robbed in their own home—it was too hard to locate in the first place, and they had nothing of value to take. Although rumours being what they are, I'm sure some thought they might have a treasure trove hidden on the premises. Maurice was too strong a believer in banks for that.

"But," he would say, "what happens if somebody breaks in on you? How are you going to defend yourself if all your guns are locked away?" I don't think he thought it was a real problem, but he was making a point with a hypothetical question and I agreed. I have enough problems with keys under normal conditions—I'm quite sure I couldn't find the key or unlock the gun cabinet if someone were holding a gun on me.

But his point was that our government wanted complete control over all the arms in the country, but would only succeed in having control over the ones owned by honest people.

Albertans in general, and rural Albertans in particular, see owning a gun as a God-given right. Guns are important in protecting livestock from varmints, be they little ones like gophers or bigger ones like cougars. As well, Maurice and Harold, having earned a living earlier in their lives with traps and rifles, weren't going to give them up without a fight.

"The criminal will have the advantage." Maurice pounded this point home over and over again. I don't think he was ever afraid for himself but he was genuinely concerned over the direction this country, his country, was taking.

Chapter 55

THOUGHTS ON WELFARE

"Everybody wants something for nothing," Maurice often said, and he disapproved, saying, "The only things worth having are the things you earn for yourself." I had to agree, but, as I pointed out more than once, "It's hard to see others getting free handouts when you know that it's your work and your dollars that are paying for those hand-outs." Eventually I agreed with him that it is better not to compromise oneself for a mess of potage, but if one is hungry it is certainly tempting and I could prove it with Scripture.

Maurice had been hungry more than once, and he agreed with the philosophic saying, "Offer a hungry man a choice between freedom and a sandwich, and he'll take the sandwich every time." After his death, and after talking to Clarence Smith who had opposing views on welfare, I wished the two of them had talked together on the topic and that I had been there to listen.

Maurice had an open mind and some of the best political discussions I have ever had, I had with Maurice King. Harold would sit there listening and rarely offer an opinion except, "Not going to change anything by sitting here talking about it." That was true, but at least we identified the problems and enjoyed the talks.

One other topic we discussed at great lengths, over and over again, was the Patty Hearst case. We finally decided that, yes, she could have been brainwashed to the extent she claimed; that if you keep pounding on a person mentally, verbally, eventually that person will agree with you, follow you and do everything you say.

We had begun on this one thinking that it was impossible, but both of us changed our minds. Maybe we were brainwashing each other.

Chapter 56

ONE SMALL FLOWER

*M*aurice had always been a generous contributor to the little Anglican Church of St. Martin's, even before the new building went up by the Waldron Bridge and the old one was moved to Heritage Park in Calgary. He was a believer—they both were. They honestly believed that their rigorous lifestyle and their lack of greed for material comforts was the best way to live.

Heavily in debt for most of their adult lives, Maurice honestly believed that he was still following Biblical advice—only to borrow for land. He knew his Bible well, and so did I. We had many good conversations based on religion, Biblical laws, government laws and religious institutions and practices.

He was ahead of me in one area, that of the King James Version of the Bible. "Can't believe these new versions of the Bible," he would say. "Stick to the King James Version because they keep changing things to suit themselves today." He was right. After he had died, I had to buy a new translation of the Bible for a Religious Studies course I was taking and I was amazed at the liberties that had been taken and the changes made. Later I got out a different translation and compared it also with the King James Version and I did not entirely approve, either.

The woman, who after his death claimed squatter's rights to the shack where she had lived and the land it was on, said that she and Maurice often read the Bible together. I wonder what version they read. I don't know how anyone can have squatter's rights on land somebody else already owns but she apparently claimed them. How Maurice could read, either, when he could hardly see, I don't know. His cataracts were so bad.

Maurice was aware of the changes at the little pan abode church of St. Martin's at the Waldron Bridge. He knew that most of its members had quit coming and that its days were numbered. It could not have survived as long as it did without his annual contributions. We often phoned to see if he would like to attend the annual Thanksgiving service and dinner there and he usually said yes. Dressed in his best blue jeans and flannel shirt, he would come with us and seemed always to enjoy the occasion. I would see that he got down the basement stairs after the service and got sat at one of the tables put up for the occasion. He never had to line up for the buffet as I fixed him a plate full of good things and took it to him. Maurice liked his food and was lucky enough to be able to enjoy it to the last.

He never used a cane, either, right till the last. All those years of walking had strengthened his legs. He did not step out in his nineties with the same firm stride he had had in earlier years but he still walked alone, literally and figuratively.

But, at the end of his life, that one small flower he picked in his final spring, and held to his face meant more to him than all the sermons he had ever heard, or than all his wealth.

Chapter 57

GETTING OLD

O ften during the winter when we had gone up to visit, the two old men would be sleeping sitting up in the living room, one on the couch and one on a chair close by. Sometimes when I went in, I didn't want to disturb them so would just go in and sit down on another chair waiting for them to wake. Often Bob, my husband, would say, "You sit beside Maurice so you can talk better."

That last year, our conversations were often repetitious—we had covered the same topics many times before but there was something comforting in repeating the familiar and in knowing that at least two of us shared the same views.

Sometimes I held his hand as we sat side by side. He needed the human touch and perhaps I needed to provide it. Often I thought that while he and Harold had shared their lives all those years, now, in his old age, he knew what he had missed and was seeking reassurance more than affection.

He had a fortune but it was not doing him much good and was more cause for worry than anything else. On one of our last visits before he went into hospital during his last illness (he had cancer) we sat at the table and suddenly he said, "I made a new will three days ago." I didn't want to discuss it. I didn't want to know what was in it or why he had changed it. But his executor told me later that he had made three or four wills in the last few months of his life and the executor wasn't sure that he really understood what he was doing or signing.

When the court case involving the squatter was going to trial, a lawyer phoned me to see if I could offer any information. I couldn't begin to see how the case even got to court as this woman hadn't a shred of evidence in writing to support her claim. All I was able to tell the lawyer, both times he phoned, was that it didn't sound like Maurice to promise anybody anything at that stage and not put it in writing. He had learned an expensive lesson in that other court case earlier, and he was nobody's fool.

But it has always puzzled me that Maurice would have taken in someone who had horses to pasture because Forestry policy is pretty strict on that point—if you can afford to give pasture to someone else, then you don't need Forestry permits.

Chapter 58

GAMBLING

I have never heard it said that Augustus King was a gambler, but very often drinking and gambling go hand in hand. Maurice only gambled on land, gambling that it would appreciate in value. As long as he was alive, he won.

But he disapproved strongly of all other forms of gambling and was horrified that any decent government would sponsor lotteries and casinos.

"I'll bet you," he would say, which statement is a kind of gambling in itself, "that if I put every dollar that some man might spend gambling into a coffee can, at the end of a year I'd have more money in that coffee can than the man had from his winnings."

I agreed with him in spite of the fact that we had made some fairly healthy wins after investing small sums in lottery tickets. He thought they were a terrible evil and I looked on it as innocent if you could keep it under control. Some can't, but will gamble away their last dollar and then borrow more to gamble.

He agreed with my attitude that one should never gamble more than one is prepared to lose. But he always added that he didn't want to lose anything.

Chapter 59

WILLIE THIBERT

Willie Thibert was another close friend of both Maurice and Harold King. Their close friends were men like themselves who shared a love of hunting and a frugal lifestyle. Willie could appreciate exactly how tough his friends had lived when things were really bad with dry summers and hard winters.

Willie thought his friends felt alienated, originally because of their father's drinking, and later, because of the way which they, through necessity, lived. I felt that Maurice deliberately flouted social conventions at times.

Willie had known the King Brothers for a long time. He had a trap line on the reserve and Harold had the other half and they could stay with the Ranger on Indian Creek. Harold made his own snowshoes and Willie learned how and also to snowshoe from Harold.

Willie's version of their coming over the ridge in the twenties was that they had a team and a wagon, one rifle, some old traps, and some grub—flour, beans, and bacon. He liked both men and told me more than once about the $300 bridle which Harold had made from horsehair braided into leather and which had gone to Australia. Willie had great respect for both men.

I never asked Willie whether Maurice phoned him to talk or not, but Ray Scotton said Maurice might phone him about ten or eleven at night and talk for several hours.

"Did he talk about religion?" I asked Ray, and the answer was, "No, I don't believe he ever did, but we talked about everything else under the sun."

He never phoned us that late in the evening but often did about eight or eight-thirty, just as I was settling down to a good book or an evening of television with the family. Once started, it was hard to stop him and we discussed a lot of things but mostly religion. It is an intriguing topic and one could go on forever and there were times when I thought we were. If Bob answered the phone and wasn't back in about fifteen or twenty minutes, someone would creep up and mouth, "Is it Maurice?" The answer was always a nod.

He must have been lonely. Maybe those were the evenings when Harold refused to discuss anything. Sometimes Maurice said, "The Boss won't talk to me." Our conversations would literally go on for hours while we solved the problems of the ranching industry and the world. Now when the phone rings, I know it isn't Maurice and there are times when I am disappointed.

Chapter 60

PEDRO

We know what happened to Pedro. Pedro, the longhorn steer, was famous. Most ranchers dehorn their cattle at the same time they brand and Kings followed the usual practice. But either the crew wasn't as careful as it should have been or else they deliberately left Pedro. The steer had a nice set of horns and Harold took it into his head to leave him be in order to see how long the horns would grow.

Most ranchers in this part of the country sell their cattle as yearlings or two year olds. Occasionally for some reason, usually price, a cattleman will hold the animals over in the fall, hoping for a price increase, by which time they will be turning three. But not often.

Pedro was the exception. When the others got rounded up to go to sale, Pedro stayed behind and roamed the range with the younger ones. He grew to be quite large and his horns grew in proportion. He had a magnificent set, quite even and well curved. Everybody was impressed with Pedro but some of the hired help began to feel that he could be dangerous.

By the time he turned six, the impressive horns had stopped growing but they kept him on one more year just to make sure. Then Pedro went the way of all mortal range cattle, but his head

Pedro on display in the Waldron House at the Kootenai Brown Pioneer Village in Pincher Creek, Alberta.

with its horns is mounted on the wall of the living room in the Waldron House in the Kootenai Brown Pioneer Village in Pincher Creek for all to see.

I don't know whether Harold did the taxidermy work on him or not, but he was proud of Pedro in life.

Chapter 61

MODERN CONVENIENCES

So much has been said and written about Maurice and Harold having lived all their lives in poverty and without modern amenities that I must mention their electricity. When rural electrification came to their corner of southern Alberta in the early fifties, they did not sign up for it.

There were at least two reasons. First of all, they were a long distance from their closest neighbour and the cost would have been exorbitant. Secondly, they didn't feel they needed it as they already had their own system. Their system was only strong enough to power a couple of light bulbs in the house, but it was superior to the coal oil and gas lamps used by others.

The King Brothers had electricity before most of their neighbours, having installed their own. It was hydropower, engineered by Harold. About 1935, he hand dug a canal through the rocks and the dirt for several hundred yards. It was about 16 feet deep and he cribbed it like a mine shaft and then covered it again.

The water from Sharples Creek ran through the canal to a spillway below the house. There it came to a drop of about six feet onto a water wheel and generated enough power to serve them. It was ingenious but typical of the two men to "do" for themselves.

Later they got a Delco, a battery-run power plant which provided enough power to run the deepfreeze they purchased to keep Maurice's beloved ice cream, as well as a couple of light bulbs. They felt that those and a radio were all they needed.

Chapter 62

GONE BUT NOT FORGOTTEN

*K*ings have gone, both Maurice and Harold, two old men who had lived their lives together knowing that they had only each other to trust. Neither one of them would have liked the bickering and squabbling which arose over their estate. But one of the first things done after Maurice's death was something that should have been done a number of years earlier.

We nearly always drove the truck when we went to visit them as we were quite sure the car wouldn't make it over the potholes or through the mud holes. It wasn't high enough. When Maurice wondered why people didn't come to see them, Eve told him more than once that if he would build a decent road in from the main road, they would have more company. But it was not until after his death that the estate built the road.

I did not go to the auction sale where their personal effects were sold, but I understand that one of Harold's empty tobacco cans sold for a ridiculous price. They had little of real value for sale, but curiosity seekers, antique hunters, and some who were simply intrigued by the King legend, turned out in vast number to bid and buy. I could imagine Maurice chuckling over the crowd of people who had turned out to buy their backless old chairs and other useless, worthless items for far more than they had cost new.

The land sale was even better attended and made headlines in the Eastern papers as well as in Calgary and Lethbridge. My husband went with one of his brothers to the land sale, even though they had no intention of bidding.

I stayed home and remembered them. I think of the two men often and I am still not sure which hurts the most, their lives, or their deaths. They accumulated a fortune and I know that Maurice enjoyed making it more than he would have spending it. They lived the only way they knew how and as circumstances dictated. But it still seems a pity to me that when they could afford to do the things they had wanted to do in early life, they felt too old. Many people envied them their material wealth but few wanted to live like Kings to achieve it.

The spray of flowers on Maurice's casket was symbolic. The single rose in the centre represented him, and the baby's breath surrounding the rose represented the generations which followed him. Maurice was very much aware that life does not stop with the death of one person, but goes on and on. He had earned his eternal rest and I strongly feel that the words, "Gone, but not forgotten" apply to them both.

They rest side by side now but they live on in memory and I am glad I knew them.

ABOUT THE AUTHOR

*M*ary-Jo Burles is the author of several books, articles, and short stories. She has written for *The Globe and Mail*, CBC Radio, *The Family Herald*, *The Pincher Creek Echo*, and many other publications. The King Brothers were among the first people she met when she moved to Alberta as a young schoolteacher. She married a cattle rancher, raised six children, and remained in the Porcupine Hills near Cowley, Alberta.

PUBLISHER'S NOTE

*H*BLS thanks Diane Aldrich, Gillian Burles, Heather Burles, Jacquelyn Burles, Mark Burles, Mary-Jo Burles, Robert Burles, Lydia Del Bianco, Sheri Henderson, Edith Knight, Denise Lawson, Ellen Liberman, Gerd Sandrock and the Glenbow Museum Archives for their help in shaping this edition of Mary-Jo's book.